"I have known the Garcia family for t
them to be dear friends. What you will find in this book is the very reason why they are so special. Full of humor, truth, and practical wisdom, *Raising Families the Jesus Way* is a wonderful dive into the special relationship between a father, mother, daughter and son told from each of their individual perspectives. Mary, Sarah, Sal, and Frank will take you deep into just what it takes to be a loving parent and a loving child in a world that does its best to tear families apart. I highly recommend you read this book!"

—Amir Tsarfati, founder and president
of Behold Israel Ministries

"The parent-child team of Mary, Frank, Sarah, and Sal Garcia brings the focus back to God and the family in this parenting book for such a time as this."

—#1 *New York Times* bestselling author Karen Kingsbury

"Having witnessed Sarah's life since we were teenagers, I feel it's too right to share thoughts not as an artist but as her friend. Her life speaks even louder than the heartfelt text in this book. She is a woman who is loyal to her community, is passionate about Jesus and above all else honors her parents. The unquestionable fact about her work is that it is always pure and authentic."

—Moriah Smallbone, artist and writer, wife to
Joel Smallbone (For King & Country)

"I have yet to start a family of my own, but it's something I am prayerfully preparing to do with Jesus at the center. I've loved getting to see the practical application of how to do just that through the wisdom and experiences of the Garcia family. Filled with insights, challenges, and how to overcome those challenges with a God-fearing perspective, they have been a real blessing to me. Both in my life today, and in the future family I hope to raise."

—Michael Andrew, Olympic gold medalist
and world record holder

"Have you ever met a family that had an incredible culture? They were full of love, joy, and peace? The Garcia family has that, and I'm so excited about their new book. You don't have to be raised in a great family or even feel like you have an incredible culture in your family now. With their insights, you can begin to work toward building a house full of love. There is really nothing more important."

—Matt Brown, evangelist, author of
Truth Plus Love, founder of Think Eternity

"Mary, Sarah, Sal, and Frank are the truest examples of everything they write in this book. Their book is packed full of applicable truths, relevant examples at every turn and so much encouragement. This book is incredibly refreshing and will truly be a game-changer for families!"

—Masey McClain, actress in *I'm Not Ashamed*, author

RAISING FAMILIES
THE
JESUS WAY

RAISING FAMILIES THE JESUS WAY

Biblical Insights for Godly Parenting and Shaping Future Generations

Mary, Sarah, Sal, *and* Frank Garcia

Chosen

a division of Baker Publishing Group
Minneapolis, Minnesota

Published by Chosen Books
Minneapolis, Minnesota
www.chosenbooks.com

Chosen Books is a division of
Baker Publishing Group, Grand Rapids, Michigan

Printed in the United States of America

Library of Congress Cataloging-in-Publication Data
Names: Garcia, Mary, author. | Garcia, Frank, author. | Garcia, Sarah, author. | Garcia, Sal, author.
Title: Raising families the Jesus way : biblical insights for godly parenting and shaping future generations / Mary Garcia, Frank Garcia, Sarah Garcia, Sal Garcia.
Description: Minneapolis, Minnesota : Chosen Books, a division of Baker Publishing Group, [2023] | Includes bibliographical references.
Identifiers: LCCN 2022037946 | ISBN 9780800762940 (trade paper) | ISBN 9780800763169 (casebound) | ISBN 9781493439409 (ebook)
Subjects: LCSH: Parenting—Religious aspects—Christianity. | Child rearing—Religious aspects—Christianity.
Classification: LCC BV4529 .G369 2023 | DDC 248.8/45—dc23/eng/20221007
LC record available at https://lccn.loc.gov/2022037946

All interior images by Michaela Andrew. Used with permission.

Cover design by Darren Welch Design

Authors represented by the literary agency of A Drop of Ink, LLC. www.adropofink.pub.

Baker Publishing Group publications use paper produced from sustainable forestry practices and post-consumer waste whenever possible.

23 24 25 26 27 28 29   7 6 5 4 3 2 1

To the woman who embodied compassion, selflessness, strength and love to my family and me: my beautiful mother, Alicia Baez, who is now in the arms of Jesus. To my dad, who gave his life to Jesus, and together we have seen so many miracles. And to my husband, Frank, and my son and daughter, Sal and Sarah. The Lord has blessed me abundantly to have you as my family. Together, we have been through the highs and lows of life, but it has been a blessing to see us grow through the trials and ultimately grow closer together as a family. And to my beautiful Aunt Carmen, who has suffered so much, yet through her suffering she still has continually loved God and loved family. You all, including Jesus, are my world, and I am beyond blessed to write this God-ordained message with you.

To the people of every stage of life (single, engaged, married, families) who picked up this book—we wrote this book for you. I pray that through each page you would feel enlightened, encouraged and empowered to walk in the Lord and raise families the Jesus way. We pray salvation over you in the name of Jesus, a resolve to walk in the fear of the Lord, transformation of your heart and mind, a love for God's Word that will shape you and be your manual for raising families, breakthroughs over generational strongholds, courage to discipline and be the spiritual leader in the home, wisdom to unfold how God created your kids to be, and that you would be led by the Spirit in all areas of your life, show grace, and leave a legacy of faith for generations to come.

—Mary B. Garcia

CONTENTS

FOREWORD

We had the pleasure of meeting Sarah while in Israel several years ago. We were immediately struck by her grace and kindness, but the more we got to know her, we were deeply impressed by her leadership, drive, and compassion to reach the lost and forgotten.

Just recently we were honored to witness the whole Garcia family ministering together in one of the many services they lead for their ever-growing community. It's a rare thing to see a family loving Jesus and loving each other the way the Garcias do. We can assure you, there is not a better family to learn from in the ways of family life. They have done it well, following Jesus, their Shepherd and Leader, through every phase of life.

Raising Families the Jesus Way is a beautiful view of the special relationship between a mother and father, daughter and son, told from their individual perspectives. Mary, Frank, Sarah, and Sal will take you on a beautiful journey of what it takes to be a loving parent and a loving child in a world that no longer views family as a strength. One of the many highlights we so appreciate about this book is that it doesn't just focus on parenting children, but encourages parents to do the heart work on themselves first so that their children can rightly model their godly character.

Our prayer is that, as you read this book, you will feel strengthened with might by God's Spirit in your inner man, and that you would be ready to make step-by-step changes to create a legacy of faith for your children and their children to come. God bless you as you embark on this journey into the heart of Jesus for family.

Cory and Anna Asbury, Grammy nominated Christian
artist/songwriter, dad and mom

ACKNOWLEDGMENTS

by Mary B. Garcia

My husband, Frank, and I want to thank our beautiful daughter, Sarah, who encouraged me to write this book. She is such a talented writer, and her help and support, along with the help of the Holy Spirit, is the only reason why this book is here today. Thanks to Sarah for pouring her heart and soul into this book. Her obedience to God's call will be greatly rewarded here on earth and into eternity.

We want to thank our wonderful son, Sal. He took on so many different roles to help get this book published. He put his mind to it and quickly became our resident graphic designer, content editor, grammar inspector, theology examiner, photographer, videographer, podcast producer, IT manager, idea gatherer, and movie reference extraordinaire. Thanks to Sal for giving his whole heart and mind to this book, using his gifts and talents for the Lord as he has always done.

We want to acknowledge the Chosen Books and Baker Publishing Group team who worked so hard on getting this book out. From the executives to the editors and marketing and design teams—thank you all so much. It was a team effort, and working with you was a joy and an honor. A special thanks to David Sluka, Jill Olson, and Hannah Ahlfield—our editors at Chosen Books. They took such special care of the content of this book, and they were always there for us on this writing journey to answer all of our questions.

And a very special thanks to our amazing, incredible, talented, kindhearted agent—Tom Dean. There are obviously not enough adjectives to describe what an extraordinary person he is. Not only is he an incredible agent to work with, but through this whole process, he became family. He loves deeply and was always there to help us in this journey, and even to pray with us through the trials. He worked tirelessly to get us a publishing deal and oversaw so many of the details that really brought this book into fruition. We're beyond blessed to know him and to have worked with him.

Thank you to the numerous friends and family who came alongside us to pray with us through the writing process. Their support and love meant the world.

Those we've named here and so many more unmentioned have all enriched our lives beyond measure. May the Lord continue to pour blessings upon each and every one.

PART ONE

THE ESSENTIALS

1

BACK TO THE BIBLE

God's "E-manual" for Parenting

Do you ever wish you could be Marty McFly, and just hop in your DeLorean, travel to the future, and see how your kids turn out—just like in the movie *Back to the Future*? I don't know one parent who wouldn't love to have that kind of foreknowledge, to have all the guesswork and stress taken out of parenting. Parents are always coming up to me, and asking questions like, "Do you think I am disciplining my kids too much or too little? Do I make them obey me, or do I give them more freedom?" Let's face it, no one wants to mess up parenting so badly that Doc Brown shows up from the future in a DeLorean, hollering, "Something's gotta be done about your kids!" This book is designed to give that after-the-fact insight. Coming from the various perspectives of our whole family—mother, father, daughter, and son—you get the parenting lessons, followed by the insights from the adult children who received those lessons. A holistic perspective, a true collaboration, thirty years in the making.

Why is it that every other song you hear these days has an artist, featuring another artist, featuring a DJ? There is power in collaboration. We wanted this book to be different from the other parenting and family life books that are out there by giving you four different perspectives. My husband and I will provide the experience of thirty-plus years of parenting, and my daughter and son will give honest insights into what it was like growing up under that experience, what our parenting looked like through their eyes. Together, we offer you a Holy Spirit–inspired manual on how to raise Christlike children who are rooted and grounded in the Word, who will carry that foundation forward to shape generations to come. Since my daughter and I are counselors, we will also give you much-needed tools to help you lay the groundwork in your own heart and mind first, so that your children can rightly model your character and actions.

This book won't take you back to the future, but back to the Bible for a foundational big picture of what family and parenting are all about. We desire to give you God's wisdom, understanding, vision, motivation, and renewed strength. We hope to help you find God's perspective of all He has for you. We start by giving you a clear understanding of who you are in the task of family and parenting, and then who the children are whom God has entrusted to you.

God has given me a vision to stop treating symptoms but get to the root of family and parenting problems. When you go to a good doctor, they won't just give you pharmaceutical medicine to temporarily relieve the symptoms, but rather they will ask questions about your daily activities, family history, how much natural sunlight you're getting, your gut microbiome, your daily food log, and they'll take your blood work. Hippocrates is believed to have said, "The greatest medicine of all is teaching people how not to need it." If we get back to Bible basics first and start with the heart of parenting, we will be able to lay a strong foundation upon which we can build effective parenting strategies.

Meeting Jesus

I'd like to start off by telling how Jesus saved my life and grafted me into His family. You might not believe this story, but it really did happen—all of it.

The year was 1979 and I was eighteen years old (if you are doing the math on my age, stop right there please). I was a first-generation American living in Los Angeles. My family grew up in poverty, and to make matters worse, my father (who is now Christian and doesn't mind me sharing his testimony) had a drinking problem, which created a lot of chaos and trouble in the home. My family was Catholic, but by that I mean we went to mass a few times a year just so we could call ourselves Catholic. We were what I like to call a CEO family (Christmas-Easter-Only). Because religion was somewhat a part of my life, I knew about God, but I really didn't *know* God or have a personal relationship with Him. My life was falling apart from the inside out when the enemy started infiltrating my mind with suicidal thoughts. One day as I drove in my car around a winding California freeway, I heard a voice in my head tell me that if I simply turned the wheel of my car so it went off the cliff, all the pain would go away . . . everything would be right and peaceful. I cried out loud in a choked voice, "Jesus! If You're really real, if You actually love me, if You actually have a plan for me—please show me!" Right at that moment, I heard a loud *honk*. I looked out my driver window and saw a car with four passengers. All four were men that looked exactly the same, and they were glowing! They looked over at me, smiled, and then each of them held up a little sign that said the same thing: *Jesus Loves You.* They waved the signs at me and then, just as quickly as they appeared, drove off into traffic. I pulled over onto the side of the road and sat for what seemed like forever—eyes wide, mouth open in amazement. Then, the tears started as I realized the truth that it brought: It wasn't just some crazy vision. Jesus was real! He loved me and had literally just saved my life! He heard my prayer and brought what I believe were angels to intervene.

After that life-altering experience I started to attend a local Christian church that my teacher from school had been inviting me to. And it was in that local Bible-teaching church that I gave my life to Christ. I started to read the Bible for the first time, and realized that in Christ, I am now part of the family of God. God is my heavenly Father and I am His daughter. He adopted me, He redeemed me, He saved me! A new Mary was born, and I could feel the joy and the peace of Jesus transforming my heart and mind.

Thinking back on that pivotal moment in the car, I now realize the significance of the four passengers in the car that day.
God was foreshadowing His plans for my life. He would one
day bless me with an amazing husband and twins. Together,
we would become a family of *four*.

You might be thinking, "Great Scott! Is that story true?" It
absolutely is, and it's why I am so passionate about my family.
Because Jesus saved me and adopted me into His family. He
showed me why I needed to continue living here on earth—to
raise a family that would love Jesus and be world changers. And
that together, we could bring you this book on family.

Going Deeper

Life is all around us. We see it in the wonder of trees as they
photosynthesize and give us our oxygen. We see it in the rolling
hills of green and groves that birth succulent fruit. All this wonder and whimsy comes into fruition (*fruit*-ion) by one single itsy-
bitsy thing we call a seed. If a seed holds so much power, you'd
think it would have some responsibility, right? After all, with
great power comes great responsibility (Spider-Man's Uncle Ben
taught us that). Seeds have the responsibility to make sure they
turn into the right plant or tree. But how do they know exactly
what to turn into? The answer to this fantastic question is this:
Inside of each seed there is a blueprint called DNA. When the
seed is planted in the ground, its DNA gives instructions about
when to grow, what to develop, and how to carry out all the
chemical reactions and biological processes it needs in order to
become a plant and stay alive.[1] There is a unique DNA blueprint
for each and every one of the millions of living organisms out
there. Pretty cool, huh?

Just like seeds have their own unique DNA blueprint, so does
the Word of God have its blueprint for your child's life. And as

you unfold the blueprint of God's Word, what does it reveal? It reveals the root system that is foundational for your children to grow into Christlikeness and bear good fruit. If you've ever grown your own plant before, you know it's a slow process. It seems like forever before the plant finally rears its head above the soil. But if you take a look under the surface, you'll see that the plant has been doing a lot of work out of sight. It has grown an intricate root system that will sustain life for itself and keep it rooted in the ground as it grows bigger and taller. Parenting is a slow, steady growth. You only have about eighteen years to set that solid, foundational root system in your child's life before they're off on their own.

There are so many great resources out there on parenting, but many of them focus on behavior (the fruit) rather than getting down to the root system, or even further down, to the seed's DNA code. What's so amazing about the Christian life is that once a person is born again, the Holy Spirit comes inside them, and they go from being dead in sin to alive in Christ. They begin the process of regeneration into the image of Christ through the transformational work of the Holy Spirit. The *implanted* Word of God goes deep down into the soil, changing the heart and renewing the mind from old patterns of thinking. God has given the Word to us in order to change us—so that we, as parents, can raise Christlike children. It is glorious that the Word of God, like a seed with the information coded in it, will make us like Jesus. In essence, it all comes down to this: If you change the code, you'll change the fruit. That's what we want to do in this book. We want to get back to what the Word of God says about raising children and how that can be coupled with the transformational work of the Holy Spirit in our lives and our children's lives.

In the Bible, *seeds* always refer to the Word of God, and the Word of God is Jesus (see John 1:1). Therefore, when we point our children to Jesus and exemplify Christlikeness in our lives to them, we are enabling them to grow in the grace and knowledge of Jesus. It all comes down to *Jesus*. This is why everything that we talk about in this book will point back to Jesus. Jesus is the key to unlock the "grow code." And the manual to follow is the Word of God. Let's take a look.

Back to the E-manual

When our twins (son Sal and daughter Sarah) were born, I remember looking at the daunting task before me and feeling completely overwhelmed. My twins were a miracle from God from the beginning because, for the longest time, doctors told me that I couldn't have kids. You can imagine how unprepared I was when I became pregnant with not just one, but two! Also, I'm a woman of small stature, so carrying two human beings was quite a feat. All throughout my pregnancy, I focused on the goal of birth. All I wanted was two healthy babies. But after they were born and we returned home from the hospital, my husband and I looked at each other, looked at the babies, and both said rather comically, "Now what?" It's a little like getting a new electronic gadget and not having a manual, or bringing home IKEA furniture that you have to assemble from scratch (minus the Swedish names and funny stick figures). God bless IKEA and their low prices, but you get what you pay for, which includes hours of labor and racking your brain trying to assemble parts seemingly designed to make your life more difficult.

Our twins didn't come with a manual or a 1-800 number in case we had questions if something went wrong. I remember praying, "God, You love us so much, You didn't create us just to let us figure things out on our own." No, that's not the God that He is. He did, in fact, give us a manual for life—the *Bible*. God's perfect Word was revealed to us, and anything that we need to know about ourselves is in it. The name Emmanuel means "God with us." God gave us an "E-manual" to be with us every step of the way. Jesus and His Word, working through the help of the Holy Spirit, is our *Emmanuel*—God with us!

Psalm 119:105 (NKJV) says, "Your word is a lamp to my feet and a light unto my path." The Word is a light that is shining our way—shining in the darkness of this world to guide us where we need to go, to let us know who we are, why we are here, who we are supposed to serve, and what God's will is for our lives. God is so amazing. Through His Word (our manual), He gives us instructions on how to guide our children and how to parent. God loves us so much that He says, "I know this is a daunting task, but I am with you and in you to guide you—and I will give you My Word to show you the way." Remember, God loves your kids more than you love your kids.

Our children are God's children. We're only stewards of them; we don't own them. He's lending them to us to raise in His path and in His ways. This mindset casts out all fear and shame when it comes to parenting. Why? Because anything you fear or are shameful of means you still own it. Give your kids over to God and let Him be the rightful owner. It's the most freeing thing you can do as a parent. We see this in Psalm 127:3 (NKJV): "Behold, children are a heritage from the LORD, the fruit of the womb is a reward."

I didn't know how to parent when I started my family. My father was a responsible man and took care of us, but he had a drinking problem that got in the way of a stable family life. My mother did her best. I believe her great love for us was what carried us through. She would pray and ask God to help her, and God, in His grace, was there with us. But there was something missing. We needed the Word of God to guide us.

In short, my husband and I didn't know how to raise a family the Jesus way, so we looked to God and said, "Okay, Father

God, please show us Your Word that would help us understand how we're supposed to guide and raise up our children." We had to let go of our pride and opinions and see what God said about family. We asked God to guide us, and that's what He did. He showed us how to raise our children through the guidance of His Word and the help of the Holy Spirit. Now, my husband and I still messed up—in fact, we messed up often. The things we did wrong we are now passing on to you so that you won't have to make the same mistakes that we did. We hope that our testimony will encourage you to believe that all things are possible with God in your life.

My husband is a pastor and construction business owner, so he knows a thing or two about building on a solid foundation. He will tell you that if the foundation is not solid, then the whole structure is at risk. We need to build a parenting foundation on the Word of God (our E-manual). The task of raising little human beings is huge, but God is the One who let us conceive and give birth—that means He will show you how to guide them every step of the way. Trust Him. He is with you.

As you can see, this book is not your typical "Top Ten Tips to Tame Toddler Temper Tantrums" kind of parenting book. By the end, we hope you will see the heart and mind of your child transformed through powerful, life-changing biblical concepts.

So, hop into your DeLorean, buckle your seat belt, and hold on, because you're about to embark on a journey that will forever change this thing we call parenting.

2

ESSENTIALS FOR PARENTING THE JESUS WAY

Foundations for Godly Parenting

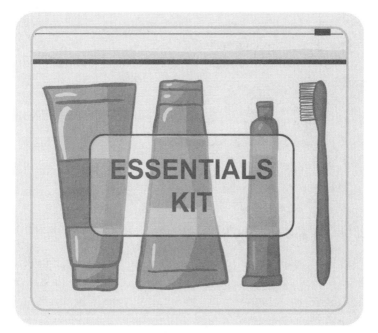

Raise your hand if you've heard of the comedian Brian Regan. If you haven't, go look him up right now. He is one of our favorite comedians because his comedy is clean and downright hilarious. In one of his acts, he talks about a time when he had the misfortune of going through what every flyer dreads—losing your luggage at the airport. I remember walking up to the lost luggage claim a few years ago and calmly stating my situation. The lady at the counter assured me that they would find my luggage and deliver it to me at my hotel. In the meantime, she offered me an "essentials kit" that included toothpaste, toothbrush, and floss. Apparently, they really care about your dental health. If these were the only essentials I needed, then I had definitely overpacked. The essentials kit reminds me of healthy parenting. There are countless books out there with hundreds of ways to parent your child—so much so that we can get overwhelmed and, in a sense, overpack. But all we need are a few necessities. God makes it simple. Just like the Gospel.

There are four essentials for laying a solid foundation for raising children:

1. Having a strong and healthy soul
2. Having an ambassador mindset
3. Building the family on the Word
4. Preparing your child's heart for salvation

A Strong and Healthy Soul

This book is all about raising families the Jesus way. But what does it mean to walk in the way of Jesus? It means to have a healthy fear of the Lord, which in turn creates a healthy soul. That's where this book starts. The focus is not on how to become a better parent, but instead, the focus is on Jesus (the Way), and the outcome is a healthy soul, marriage, and family, as well as peace in the nation. Psalm 128 says this:

> Blessed are all who fear the LORD, who walk in obedience to him.
> You will eat the fruit of your labor; blessings and prosperity will be yours.
> Your wife will be like a fruitful vine within your house; your children will be like olive shoots around your table.
> Yes, this will be the blessing for the man who fears the LORD.
> May the LORD bless you from Zion; may you see the prosperity of Jerusalem all the days of your life.
> May you live to see your children's children—peace be on Israel.

What God is saying here is that in order to have peace in the nation and impact the world for generations to come, there first needs to be a healthy soul. So what does it mean to have a healthy soul? It means fearing the Lord. Now the word *fear* here does not mean a spirit of fear or being afraid, but rather it means a holy fear. This type of fear is reverential. It is about being in awe of the greatness and power of God. It's a revelation that God is so mighty and powerful, yet He packaged all that up to become a man and die on the cross for your sins. That kind of grace and love is not to be taken lightly. It is often overwhelming, even to the point that it leads you to offer your body as a living sacrifice to the Lord and walk in the way of Jesus (see Romans 12:1). This is what it looks like to have a healthy soul that fears the Lord.

Points of view (POVs) are the popular things to post on social media right now, so try this for a point of view: Your family does not begin when you have children, but rather, when you and your spouse are joined together in marriage. That is when your family journey begins, when your family "boat" starts sailing. So that should be when you and your spouse are collectively aiming to have healthy souls, walk in the fear of the Lord, and serve the Lord together. That way, when children do come, they can simply hop on the boat and join you down the river toward God. Levi Lusko, pastor and author, says that when you start with the foundation of anchoring your heart in the fear of the Lord and resolve out of that fear to live a life that pleases Him, the outcome is that you will see God's blessing in your marriage, your children, and the world.[1]

An Ambassador Mindset

As Christian parents, we are called to be *ambassadors* to our children: to represent the purposes, character, and methods of God. An ambassador does not ask, "How can I mold my children into what I want them to be?" but rather, "What does God desire in the lives of my children, and how can I be part of it?" He's giving them to you for a season so that you can mirror His image to them, disciple them, and represent who God truly is in the midst of a secular world. Sometimes we put so much of a burden on ourselves, thinking that we are our children's owners and that we ultimately will take on the full responsibility if they grow up to be bad or good. Remember— you are only an ambassador. When I came to this realization in my own parenting, it took a huge load off my shoulders. The main thing that I have to do is simply lead my children to the Lord. Like John the Baptist, all I have to do is be a signpost, pointing my kids to Jesus by the way I live my life and by teaching them the Word.

We, as parents, need to embrace our complete inability to change the hearts and lives of our kids. We need to recognize our role as *tools* in the hands of the One who alone has the power to create lasting change. First Corinthians 3:6 puts it this way: "I planted the seed, Apollos watered it, but God has been making it grow."

Parenting is an art, not a science. It sanctifies us, challenges us, and blesses us. But the beauty of parenting is that God gave you specifically to your children. Don't be hard on yourself. Don't live in guilt. Don't always be thinking that everything you do wrong will eventually send your kids into therapy. Maybe you've heard it before: There are a million ways to be a good parent, but there's no way to be a perfect one. Just do your best.

Having success in parenting will require relational connection. Just be there for your kids. Be present. Love them the best way you can—pray and rely on the Holy Spirit to guide you and guide them. One thing that may surprise you: God trusts you. Even seeing all your mistakes and shortcomings, He still entrusted you with parenting these children, specifically. So rest in the beauty of that truth. As cheesy as it sounds, it's so true: Do your best and God will do the rest. It's okay to mess up. It's okay to lose your child at Costco because you got distracted by the honey barbecue bacon-wrapped shrimp samples. Feel the gravity and the weight of being a great parent, but also live in the freedom and the grace to not have it all together all the time. This is a season for planting—later on you'll see the growth. You don't have to be a perfect farmer. Consistency, not perfection, is the key.

Your calling and your purpose as a parent are summed up in one word: *redemption*. Your children need to be redeemed. That can only happen through God Himself. Your task is to know Him and make Him known to your kids. We will talk more about salvation later.

Insights from Sarah

I had a tendency of not telling the whole truth growing up (I probably should have paid more attention to that VeggieTales video *LarryBoy & the Fib from Outer Space!*). My parents would often have to sit me down and tell me how speaking half truths was not good and then give me the Word of God that shows why it's wrong. Over and over they would tell me and discipline me—yet I still kept justifying it by thinking it wasn't a blatant lie, so I was okay. Until the day I felt a real tug and conviction in my spirit that what I was doing was not only grieving my parents, but grieving Jesus. It was like a light bulb finally went on in my mind and reached my heart. I went to my parents and apologized and told them I didn't want to do it anymore. My parents praised God because they knew that the consistency of feeding me the truth and following up with discipline had finally paid off. Parents, you might feel like you're spinning your wheels. You might feel like you are on a crazy cycle of lecturing and conversing, then disciplining and teaching, and it's not going anywhere. Be encouraged: God's Word never returns void. Keep taking your children back to Scripture as my parents did for me. This watering and pruning is as important as growth, because it sanctifies and prunes *parents*. It gets you in Scripture. It works patience in you. It empties you of selfishness. It helps you rely entirely on the Holy Spirit. God is working in you and in your children at the same time. He's the ultimate multitasker.

Family: The Key to Change

I know there are many wonderful families in our country right now. There are parents who have taught and directed their children well. There are young married couples just starting out. And there are single parents working to raise and direct their children in the nurture and admonition of the Lord that Ephesians 6:4 directs. Still, there are many problems facing our nation today, and those problems did not occur overnight—they have been getting progressively worse with each generation. In the 1950s, teachers reported the main problems that were occurring in the schools were damaged books, running in the hallways, and spitballs (ah yes, the good ol' days). Now, the main problems teachers have in the schools are teenage pregnancies, drugs, and mass shootings. Yikes! What on earth happened?

For one, when you take God out of the public schools and start teaching kids that they came from animals, they're likely going to start acting like animals. When you start teaching them they merely came from primordial slime, they are going to start doing slimy things. Another huge factor that started to expedite the decline of our society was a sect in the feminist movement that happened in the 1960s and began to dismantle the nuclear family. Now, there's nothing wrong with a "career woman," but when her career comes at the expense of the children, then that's where the problem starts. When we look at history we see that a certain part of this movement was against the nuclear family. Moms started to leave their children to be "raised" by the school system and their peers. Losing the role of the mother, especially in homes with already absent fathers, takes away a needed foundation and continues to create generations that are rebellious and worldly at heart.

With a culture that is binary and divided, God calls the family to be united—which is why the family has been under attack by the enemy. The enemy knows that the family not only represents the image of Christ but is the key to restoring and reforming nations. If the mother and father knew the importance of their God-given responsibility to discipline and raise their children in the Lord, then our nation today would be facing a lot less problems. *The family is the key to shifting the culture.*

The world has had a lot to say over the years about what it thinks family is. The abundance of intentional pregnancies of single women, especially celebrities, has sent the message that children don't need fathers. Men are made fun of for their masculinity. In years past, wives and mothers have not been given the honor they deserve, either. All of these ideas, believe it or not, are being indoctrinated into our kids through the school system, social media, and entertainment. We need to reprogram our children's minds and model what a godly family looks like. This means we need to go back to God's Word to rebuild the family—that is our purpose and calling as parents.

Author and pastor Tony Evans, in his book *One Family Under God*, teaches that Nehemiah rebuilding the wall of Jerusalem is a powerful illustration of family. "God's chosen people are going through a national, cultural, and family crisis," Evans wrote. "The society is in despair, wasting away. Their captors had torn down Jerusalem's defensive walls, and the people of Israel had been living in exile for 150 years. During this critical time, God raised up two men who were willing to lead their people from physical ruin." Nehemiah 4:14 says, "Don't be afraid of them. Remember the Lord, who is great and awesome, and fight for your families, your sons and your daughters, your wives and your homes." Evans continues, "God put a fire in Ezra's and Nehemiah's hearts to lead His chosen people and to urge them to fight for their families. Nehemiah and Ezra understood that in order to repair a broken society, you must not only rebuild the walls, you must rebuild the people. . . . Lasting change must occur in individual hearts and in homes."

So as our country continues further from God's intended order, Satan's plan grows, Evans said. "Just like the devil had a plan in the garden of Eden, he has a plan in the garden of America today. And the primary target of this plan is the family. As goes the family, so goes the nation."[2]

Satan targets the family because the family holds the key to change society. It is both *through* and *within* the family that children and leaders are created and matured. This is why, more than ever, it is the family's role to take back those places of influence. Gone are the days of obsessing over building our career, or the number of people in our church, while the world and its systems are raising our children instead of us. You must be present for your children. Make them your top priority (more than career or ministry or working out). Spend the majority of your time with them, especially in their younger years. Saturate them with the Word. Model Christ to them. Take mission trips together. Establish discipline, nurture, and structure.

Author and speaker Nate Johnson shared this powerful commission for families.

> If you are wondering what to build—build family. Repair family. Champion the family. Fight for the family. That's why the enemy is warring so hard after the family and the values of kingdom family because he sees that it is the future.

He goes on to say that the enemy knows that the gateway to shifting the pendulum in our culture toward the things of the Kingdom is family. Take a stand against the enemy. Tell him that he will no longer tear down your home. And you will no longer make religion your idol. The enemy has been doing a lot of teaching while we have just been preaching. He has been teaching kids through media while we have been "busy" doing things for God. We attend spiritual meetings and events, all while letting entertainment desensitize our kids to the Spirit. We must build up our homes and lead our families into the presence of God, fostering an environment where they can have real encounters with Jesus.[3]

The Road to Salvation

The most important thing you can do as a parent is to prepare your child's heart to receive Christ and to stand before God. Getting them into college is good, but getting them into heaven is better. Prepare your children for salvation and prioritize the winning of their souls to Jesus Christ. God Himself has entrusted you with introducing your (His) children to who He is and helping them establish a relationship with Him. We do our best to bring our children to God, because He sent His only begotten Son to us. He could have sent angels, or someone else, but He sent the highest love possible when He sent Himself (His Son, Jesus, and His Holy Spirit). When your children are babies, they trust you completely. They trust you to feed them, to care for them, and to do everything they need for them. In the same way, we can trust our Father God to completely take care of us and guide us in the responsibilities He gives us.

Throughout this book, you will see this recurring theme: We are just instruments in His hands. God the Father, His Son, and the Holy Spirit do the work to give your children new hearts and minds.

If you are wondering how to approach that conversation with your children, look up Bill Bright's four spiritual laws.[4] They provide a great outline for communicating the salvation message. They're simple but powerful!

If your children are old enough to understand this message and have not yet received Jesus into their hearts, share this Good News with them! Salvation, and the Holy Spirit's work of regeneration, is of the utmost importance for building a strong and biblical parenting foundation.

Applying this book to your life will be really hard to do if you don't already have a personal relationship with Jesus. We are sinners and *need Jesus*. He is at the center of all life, and the Bible is our source of absolute truth. Without the Holy Spirit guiding our lives and without God's Word, we are directionless. If you are not a child of God—if you have not received Him in faith—make that choice now! Pray this prayer:

Heavenly Father,
   Forgive my sins. Jesus, save me, make me new, fill me with Your Spirit so I can follow You, walk with You, and live for You. Show me Your love in all that I do. My life is not my own; I give it to You.
   In Jesus' name, amen.

If you just prayed that prayer, welcome to the family of God! After salvation, there is nothing that can separate us from the love of God. Nothing can snatch us from the Lord's hands. This is a great rest for us as parents. Some children don't have a true conversion until they are older, or when they go through a very heavy trial. But keep praying and believing for your children—God is faithful!

Get on Board and Your Family Will Too

Hebrews 11:7 says, "By *faith* Noah, when warned about things not yet seen, in holy fear built an ark to save his family" (emphasis added). Noah expected that his whole family would be saved. The same was true for the Philippian jailer that Paul ministered to in Acts 16. He got saved, and his whole family followed him. As parents, this is the kind of faith that we should have for our children or our future children. When we accept Jesus as our Lord and Savior and we walk in His ways, we need to believe by faith our family will follow our lead. Faith in action will change the trajectory of your whole house.

Summary of the Good News

God loves you. He proved that thousands of years ago. God became a man—Jesus Christ. He suffered and died on the cross to save *us*. He literally died to take your punishment and my punishment upon Himself so that we could be forgiven and set free from our sin. When Jesus rose from the dead and ascended to heaven, He defeated death and hell. He offers you and me eternal life. If you're willing, God can save you. Confess your sins and put your faith in Jesus Christ.

It's imperative that this foundation of salvation is laid before we begin our parenting journey. Now, let's begin.

PUT IT INTO PRACTICE: REBUILDING YOUR FAMILY ON THE WORD

- Take big events that happen in your everyday family life and bring the Word into them. For example, your little one touched the stove and burned their finger even when you told them not to touch it. Show them that's how the Bible works—the Father tells us not to do something, not to suck the fun out of everything, but to protect us from things He knows will destroy and hurt us. Your taking time to bring the Word in while their finger is throbbing will be forever ingrained in their minds. Just be sure to give them the compassion and love they need after the pain too.

- Memorize Scripture together and make it into a game. Read a psalm or a proverb together in the morning while eating breakfast or while on the way to school. Minister to your family with the Word every chance you get.

PART TWO

THE PARENT SECTION

3

YOU DO IT,
THEN YOU TEACH IT

Lead by Example by Modeling Christ

was scrolling through a streaming service one Friday night and came across a TV show called *No Good Nick*. I normally don't watch TV shows, so I was about to scroll right past it until I saw that the one and only Sean Astin was part of the cast. You know Sean Astin—the actor who played Sam in *The Lord of the Rings* and helped Frodo destroy the ring at Mount Doom and bring peace to Middle-earth (nerd alert, I know). I immediately became intrigued and clicked on an episode to see what it was about. One of the family members had left the garage door open overnight, and a lot of the dad's expensive equipment in the garage ended up getting stolen. The scene shows the dad (Sean Astin) in the garage filling out an insurance claim when his daughter walks up and peers at his paperwork. She looks puzzled and asks him why he's including a flat-screen TV and a mountain bike—things they don't actually have. The dad responds, "They don't know that. Everyone fibs on insurance claims. Insurance companies almost expect you to do it." I almost lost it. I slammed my laptop down and began writing this chapter. What pushed my buttons was what too many parents do—they enforce rules for their kids, to tell the truth and to show integrity, but they do not live it themselves. What the dad in this scene did was indirectly teach his daughter to lie and manipulate to get ahead in life.

If you want to have authority with your children, it boils down to a simple principle—*you do it, then you teach it*. In real life, if the dad in this scene would have tried to teach his daughter about integrity and honesty, it would have come to no avail, because he wasn't living it. That's why our Lord Jesus moved with incredible authority in the gospels. He was not just teaching theoretically; He actually lived out the Word. He's the Word that became flesh.

As parents, we need to be doers of the Word. As you do the Word, it gives you authority in your teaching. If your kids see that your character exemplifies honesty and integrity, you are giving them the foundation to establish truthfulness in their own lives.

Insights from Sarah

"You do it, then you teach it" was something that I saw displayed by my parents growing up. They displayed integrity and faithfulness, love and forgiveness. I remember so many instances when this played out in my life. When my dad backed into a car in a parking lot, the driver of the car wasn't there and no one was around. He could have easily left, but he chose to leave a note with his number and insurance. Or when my parents faithfully tithed to the church even when finances were tight and we were in need. They still gave, and the Lord blessed them financially down the road. They didn't just preach Malachi 3:10 to me; they lived it. My parents showed my brother and me by example that tithing brings liberation from the sinful tendency of being greedy; they showed us that it sets your heart toward heaven, because where your treasure is, there your heart will be also (see Matthew 6:21). And they also exemplified to us that tithing shows God that we can be entrusted with more of the riches of the Kingdom. They taught us that when we walk in their footsteps, we'll experience those same blessings.

Bible Story Time: Parents Leading by Example

In Judges 13, an angel of the Lord appeared to Samson's parents and gave them some good news and special instructions. He told them they were going to have a son but that they needed to follow the Nazirite code for him—he could not cut his hair and had to stay away from dead bodies and alcohol. (I get the second two, but holy moly, how long do you think his hair was by the time he was an adult? Samson must hold the record for the world's strongest man *and* the world's biggest man bun.) Samson aside, many people don't know that the angel also said that Samson's mother needed to follow the instructions of staying away from wine as well. As the story goes on, we find out that Samson broke all these rules from the get-go. His parents were walking right along with him in a vineyard. Don't get me wrong, but if you were given specific instructions from God to stay away from wine, you probably should not be wandering around a vineyard. Nonetheless, they were. This is a prime example of a mother who is relaxed in keeping God's instructions, inevitably setting up her children for temptation.

When we read the story of Samson without the context of the mother, it's easy to wonder how Samson ended up falling so badly and not staying true to who he was and how he was supposed to walk. But with the context of the mother, we see that Samson's character and failings were marred because she was not setting him up to walk in the right way by the way *she* walked. In turn, the issue is not the kid, but *you*. As a parent, you need to set a good example and stay away from unclean things. The best thing you can do for your child is to concentrate on your own walk. Titus 2:7 (NKJV) says, "In all things showing yourself to be a pattern of good works; in doctrine showing integrity, reverence, incorruptibility." First Peter 5:3 (NKJV) says, "Nor as being lords over those entrusted to you, but being examples to the flock."

Whenever we teach something to our kids, we need to be the first ones to act on it and show them by *example*. Don't be a parent that says, "Do as I say, not as I do." Lead by example. That's what Jesus did. He said to go out and make disciples and preach the Gospel, and then He did those very things. Be kind, show compassion. The God that we serve says, "You go do this because I did it first." We love Him because He first loved us. He overcame the world so we can overcome it. So give your kids that push. Say, "Guys, we are doing this, and I'm going to do it first." Show them by example. They'll say, "My parents are doing it, so I'm going to do it as well." Deuteronomy 6:4–9 says that we are to love the Lord with all our heart, soul, mind, and strength before we try teaching it, because our children are watching us. Once that is set straight, we are to teach our children the commands of the Lord, to love the Lord. Teach them at home, when they're lying down, at school, in the grocery store, everywhere. Why? Because this world will bombard them with the complete opposite. Commercials, TV, music, social media—there is propaganda everywhere that most often is steering us away from God. Instead, you need to bombard your kids with God's Truth, with the Bible. Encourage your kids to write Bible verses on cards and put them all around their room. Fill the walls of your house with Scriptures, listen to worship music, take the mundane events of the day and complement them with Scripture.

Full-Time Model

Parents are full-time models. No, you don't have to have a chiseled jawline like Henry Cavill or rock-hard abs like Ryan Gosling, but you do have to have an awareness that what you do will be absorbed and mirrored by your kids. Much more is caught than taught.

For example, if you want your kids to respect you, then you need to model that respect to them and to others. Respect cannot be taught unless it is first learned. It develops naturally. Likewise, if you don't want your kids to have temper tantrums every day, then start modeling a good temperament yourself every day. As parents, you should even model repentance. For example, if you and your spouse had an argument in front of your kids, make sure you make up in front of them as well, and apologize to them and to each other. Model humility, as well as the fear of the Lord, laughter, love, and forgiveness. The best way to teach your children is through modeling. If you consistently model respectful behavior toward family members, toward your children, and toward yourself, your children will consistently pick that up. Respecting yourself can include not allowing negative self-talk but speaking life over yourself, having high morals and convictions, and knowing your worth in Christ. Respect your body and mind as a temple of the Lord (see 1 Corinthians 6:19) by being careful what you let into your mind.

Have you ever said something in conversation like, "I'm thinking about getting a new mattress," and then the next time you picked up your phone and logged on to social media, you saw a gazillion ads about mattresses? Coincidence? I think not! Smartphone microphones are constantly collecting audio to be able to target content toward users. Some people say that the government uses this to watch and listen to you at all times. I didn't tell you this to turn you into Ron Swanson (a character on the show *Parks and Recreation* who hates the government, and at the discovery that his computer was recording his personal info, took his monitor outside and smashed it). I mentioned this as a comparison: Children are like smartphones—they're always listening, whether we realize it or not. They're like 1990s cassette tapes that keep running and recording. That's a fact.

Now the question is, what do I want to be on the tape? What do I want to be forever imprinted on my child's soul—on the tape of my child's mind? When bringing up my children, I realized early on that those tapes are recording constantly, and I want to make sure that what is recorded—what will be replayed—are things that are going to encourage, inspire, and edify, not rip off, tear down, and pollute.

Do Your Own Work

Parenting can include so much fear and guilt, especially the fear of messing up so badly that you traumatize your kids in the process. The fear-driven goal then becomes doing whatever it takes to not put your kids in a counseling chair with endless problems.

First and foremost, you need to have grace for yourself and remember that your kids' ultimate parent is God. He will take care of your kids in the long run. But the big picture starts with you. Get counseling for any inner healing that needs to take place—whether from a professional, a pastor, or a lay counselor, or through resources or books. If you have an anger problem, or are prone to anxiety, for the sake of your children if not yourself, reach out for help. Work on being disciplined in reading the Bible, praying, serving, and living worry-free.

We want people who read this book to be helped personally as much as they are helped in their parenting. Take the journey with yourself first, before starting the journey of raising your kids. Make your parenting job easier by doing the work on yourself first.

Simon Says (Modeling Christ)

Remember that old children's game Simon Says? It was a game we played growing up that would test our ability to distinguish between genuine and fake commands. You had to follow the leader whenever they led with the phrase "Simon says." For instance, they would tell the group, "Simon says, touch your nose." The leader would touch his or her nose, and the group would proceed to touch their noses. Then the leader would try to trick the group by giving a command without the key phrase "Simon says," to try to eliminate people. It was a fun game to play as a kid because kids have an innate desire to want to imitate the leader. We see this all the time with our kids. They'll come out of nowhere and start imitating us, doing things we never even realized they were observing.

Being in ministry for many years, I have discipled, counseled, and encouraged people, often on the phone. Comically, one of my habits is walking around in circles when I'm on the phone. I do this all the time around the kitchen counter—just talking and walking. When my daughter was little, she noticed my habit and started imitating me. She would randomly start walking in circles around the kitchen counter until I finally asked her, "Sweetie, why are you walking in circles?" And she replied, "I'm just doing what you do when you talk on the phone, Mommy." It is so important that we are aware of what we are "Simon saying" to our kids through our actions and our words.

Every parent wants their children to excel, but how does that happen? More influential than rigorous Bible study, playing classical music, or putting your kids through AP classes is *who you are*. This is why Paul said to the Corinthian church, "Imitate me, just as I also imitate Christ" (1 Corinthians 11:1 NKJV). Paul was so impactful in his ministry because he had a "be followers of me" mentality. He was acutely aware that people would be looking up to him, so he made sure that his actions, words, heart attitudes, and motivations were aligned to Christ: When others imitated him, they would be indirectly imitating Christ.

Like Paul, we as parents need to sit before the Lord and take inventory of what we are saying and doing. We need to daily ask the Holy Spirit to reveal anything that might be in our hearts that needs transformation, or in our minds that needs renewing. *Effective parenting is all about going private before you go public.* Going private with the Lord in prayer and in His Word, before anything else, will affect how you behave and respond that day. You'll be walking in the Spirit and personifying who He is to the world around you. Who you are privately will have the greatest impact on your children.

One practical example of this in the Bible is when Paul encourages his son in the faith, Timothy. He tells him, "Don't let anyone look down on you because you are young, but set an example for the believers in speech, in conduct, in love, in faith and in purity" (1 Timothy 4:12). Paul was telling Timothy that even though he might be unsure of his ability to preach, the most important thing was to be an example to his congregation of what a believer should be. Think about this: If everybody in your family was just like you, what would your family look like? Would they all be worry-warts? Angry time bombs? Addicted to social media? Lukewarm in their walk with the Lord? It is so important that our walk with the Lord is strong so that we can be a godly example in all that we do and say for our families. You can have family devotionals, but it's what your kids see in you personally that is going to have a lasting impact. What you do in your private life directly impacts your children's lives. Even what you do that they *don't* see will directly impact what they do in their walks. Let me give you an example from the Bible to illustrate.

Bible Story Time: Private Life Impactfulness

In 2 Samuel 21:15–22, King David and his mighty men are at war against the Philistines. A giant named Ishbi-Benob (now there's a great name for any expecting mothers reading this; Shish Kebab is another great one), who was the son of Goliath, threatens to kill David—probably wanting revenge for what he did to his dad with a sling and a stone. David's mighty men ended up coming to David's rescue and killing Ishbi-Benob,

49

along with all the other giants who were Goliath's sons. So what's the big deal? Mighty men slaying giants is rather expected (especially if you grew up on *The Lord of the Rings*). The thing is, David's mighty men weren't always mighty men. They were initially in debt, distressed, ragtag renegades. As these men began hanging around Davy the giant-slayer, they were transformed and became mighty men who slayed giants and took down Philistine armies. They became mighty in killing giants because they hung around a giant-killer. They never actually saw David kill Goliath. That was long before them. What David had previously done, personally and privately, had a direct effect on the men who were linked to him, and they became giant-killers too. Not one of Saul's men became a mighty man or a giant-killer. Do you know why? Because Saul never killed a giant himself. He was afraid of Goliath. He didn't engage in the battle, and his men were negatively influenced by that. The kids that you are raising will take on the characteristics that are truly you, even though they might not be around to watch you or know what you're up to in the spirit. You are setting the stage. You are leading the way.

If you want your child to grow up to be a man or woman of prayer, a student of Scripture, a lover of God, living fearlessly, believing and trusting God, then the most important things you can do are to pray privately, to consistently study the Word, to love the Lord, and to trust God. Who you are in secret will leave a powerful impact upon them.

In Acts 4, the Pharisees were amazed at Peter and John's knowledge and power. Like David's ragtag team who became mighty men, these men were uneducated fishermen who spent a lot of time with Jesus before being filled with the Holy Spirit and transformed into His likeness.

Your kids can learn from your strengths, and they can learn from your faults. This is why it's so important to constantly be looking inward and asking the Holy Spirit to transform and renew. If there's pride, unforgiveness, or fear in you, then it will come out in your actions and your kids will start to mirror it.

Insights from Sarah

I remember the first time my dad bought a basketball hoop for my brother and me. This basketball hoop wasn't any ordinary hoop that you hang on a garage door. It had its own base with an adjustable neck that you could lift to any height. When my brother and I tried it out, we didn't know that my dad had already adjusted the hoop to a very low height to cater to our seven-year-old statures. At that low height, shooting hoops and dunking was a piece of cake. I remember thinking, *I got this basketball thing down, baby! WNBA, here I come!* One day, a friend of ours, who was a couple of years older than us, came over to play. He saw our shortened basketball hoop and started to laugh at how low it was. He told us that if we actually wanted to get good at basketball, we were going to have to raise the rim to the standard height. He did that, and let's just say basketball got a lot harder.

The same is true for parenting. If you want your kids to walk in the fruit of the Spirit and have character, you're going to have to raise the rim in your life to that same standard of expectation. If your kids are disrespectful to you, is it because they saw you or your spouse acting disrespectfully toward each other or toward someone else? You could be reaping what you sow. You have to raise the rim with your integrity, with your speech, with your prayer, and with your quiet time with the Lord. It's going to require more energy and discipline to play, but it will be worth it.

PUT IT INTO PRACTICE:
LEADING BY EXAMPLE

- Have you ever made a daily declaration list? If you haven't, start one today. Declarations are truths that you speak over your life in order to renew your mind and keep God's Word at the forefront. A declaration list can be put on a simple note card and placed in your Bible so you can see it when you read the Word every day. For example: *I am a child of God. I am more than a conqueror in Christ. I am redeemed, loved, and forgiven.* In that list, include a declaration specific to parenting: *I will lead like Jesus, by example, and model the heart of God to my children.* When you make this a daily declaration, it will change the way you parent.

- Parenting requires a lot of *humility* and *self-awareness.* If there's sin in your life, own up to it. Deal with it, confess it, and get rid of it. Don't think it's the church's job to teach your kids how to be godly. Take a good look in the mirror: Your reflection will become their reflection. So humble yourself and fix it, so they can become what they see in you.

- Set time aside each day to pray, to be in the Word, to give, and to serve people. This will have a profound effect on who your children will become. If your daily time with God is lacking, then go deeper: Raise the rim.

4

TOO BLESSED TO BE STRESSED

Passing on a Biblical Blessing

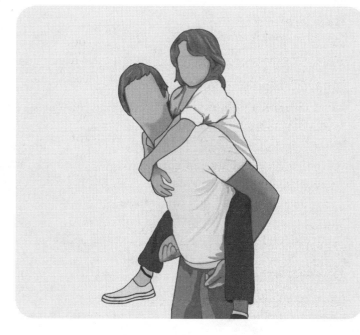

ave you ever heard the saying "too blessed to be stressed"? If you're anything like me, you've probably pinned it on a Pinterest board once or twice. It's one of those nuggets of truth that brings so much comfort and peace because it reminds us to take an inventory of all that the Lord has blessed us with, including salvation. This amazing reminder causes us to live more carefree lives with less stress. Pretty cool, huh? There's power in counting our blessings, as well as in *giving* a blessing. We're going to take a look in the Bible to see exactly how we can apply the tool of blessing over our children, and the effects that come with it.

In Genesis 27:27–29, we see that Isaac blessed Jacob (who was pretending to be Esau). In this blessing, Isaac kisses his son, he affirms his strengths, and he gives him a prophetic declaration on who he will become. As parents, the reason we need to be applying this biblical blessing to our kids is because it holds an enormous weight and importance for their future. Every child needs to have a proclamation and revelation for his or her life. They need someone to proclaim to them who they are and to give a revelation of where they're headed. That's what a biblical blessing gives to them.

Now, I'm not saying we should lay hands on our kids and say in our best Gandalf voice, "Oh, my dear child. . . . Thou art blessed, son of my womb!" Not quite. What I'm talking about is using the concepts of a biblical blessing and applying them to our children in an everyday scenario. But before we go there, let's look at another biblical blessing.

Near the end of his life, Jacob blessed Joseph's sons, Ephraim and Manasseh. He laid his hands on them and spoke words of life over them (Genesis 48:19–20). This blessing would be a foundational moment for them as they would go on to walk in that spoken calling over their lives. Later, Ephraim and Manasseh would become two of the most powerful tribes in

Israel, both economically and militarily. They ended up becoming very fruitful, just as Jacob blessed them to be.

So how can we apply a blessing to our kids in this day and age? By utilizing three components: affection, affirmation, and future direction.

Affection: The Common Denominator

In the Bible, we see a blessing was pronounced while laying a hand upon the child's head. According to *Psychology Today*, researchers have found that the absence of a father can lead to destructive behaviors in children such as delinquency, promiscuity, and teen pregnancy.[1] These children either did not have dads in their lives or had dads that rarely showed tender affection to them—like warm embraces, piggyback rides, or patting their backs. Since these women lacked tender affection from their fathers, they looked to men and physical intimacy to fill that void.

Moral of the story: It is so important for dads to consistently, lovingly, and tenderly embrace their kids. Embrace them for a whole minute without letting go and just whisper how much you delight in them and enjoy them. Such a simple embrace could be forever etched in your child's mind and heart.

Insights from Frank

When my kids were growing up, I was beyond blessed to be able to show tender affection to them. One of my favorite memories is our up-the-stairs chases. We would start at the bottom of the stairs and race to their beds. Once I said go, they would race upstairs as fast as they could, run into their bedrooms, jump in their beds and throw the covers over their heads. I would then come in a few seconds later and tickle them. We would all giggle and laugh, and I would end it with a big embrace. My kids told me that they remembered feeling euphoria during that game, and that they knew deep down in their souls that they were safe, loved, and cherished. It's amazing what a simple embrace can do. My daughter specifically told me that my tender affection to her growing up played a significant part in her not settling in relationships and saving herself for marriage. She didn't need affection from a guy because I gave that to her. Even more importantly, her heavenly Father ultimately filled that love well in her soul.

Affirmation: You Is Kind

A second way we can apply a biblical blessing to our kids is through affirmation. Biblical blessings always contained fitting words of description. For example, a child could be likened to a lion with great strength or a fruitful tree overflowing with fruit. These biblical blessings become such a powerful moment for children because through these meaningful words they gain insight into how their parents see them.

In the movie *The Help*, we see a beautiful example of this. Aibileen, a nanny and caretaker, deeply loved and cherished the little girl in her care. The mom was never attentive to the little girl and didn't even like to pick her up or hold her. The only reason she had a child was because the rest of her girlfriends were having children. She would hit the girl whenever she made even a little mistake. But afterward, Aibileen was always there to wrap the little girl in a hug and speak these words of life over her (if you know it, say it out loud in your best Viola Davis impersonation): "You is kind, you is smart, you is important." As Aibileen spoke, you could see in the girl's eyes that those simple words of affirmation brought life to her and would be a bedrock to her identity as she grew up.

Many times, we just assume our kids know that we think highly of them. But those thoughts need to be spoken. Tell them you love them on a daily basis, tell them they're kind, smart, and important. The world will be constantly speaking words of destruction over them, so that makes it all the more important to speak words of life. Words are powerful. God spoke the world into existence with words. Use them wisely and intentionally. Speak God's promises over your children and give them access to how you see them through affirmation.

Not only should we speak words of life over our kids, but we need to remember to use caution so that we are not speaking destruction. In the story of Ruth, we learn that Naomi, Ruth's mother-in-law, had two sons whose names were Mahlon and Chilion. Both names mean "sickly and pining," and they both died pretty quickly. This is not to say that's why they died, but it is cautionary for parents that what we speak over our kids is important. The Bible says your tongue has the power of life and death (Proverbs 18:21).

When someone speaks encouragement over you, it really sticks to your heart. Mark Twain said, "I can live on a good compliment two weeks with nothing else to eat."[2] Conversely, we can all remember a time in our lives when someone spoke negative things over us. Negative words can stick like Velcro on our minds and last a whole lot longer than any positive word, especially when it comes from a family member.

In the hilarious movie *Cheaper by the Dozen*, Steve Martin was the father of a family with twelve kids. The black sheep of the family was the only redhead. He was very quiet and nerdy, and he kept very much to himself. Whenever something went wrong, the siblings would blame it on him. And worst of all, they had a nickname for him: FedEx. Because FedEx must have dropped him off at the house when he was a baby, because he didn't fit in with the family. The word might have been spoken over him jokingly, but he took it to heart and ended up running away. As parents, we need to be careful. Even lighthearted nicknames like "sleepyhead" or "slowpoke," said in a joking manner, can hold weight. Take inventory of the words you speak over your kids and make sure they are words of life.

(Back to the) Future Direction!

The third component of biblical blessing is future direction. In Orthodox Jewish homes, you might hear the parents say, "Meet my son, Luke, the doctor," or, "Meet my daughter, Leia, the writer," regardless of the fact that Luke is barely seven and Leia is only five. Kids need parents to speak out in faith about what they can become, not to influence them toward a specific career, but to acknowledge their giftings and strengths. It confirms that their parents have faith in their God-given potential and purpose.

In *Back to the Future*, Marty McFly saw what his family could become if certain circumstances changed in the past. Speaking words of faith and blessing over your children can be those "certain circumstances" that change their future direction. We have the privilege of saying, "You know, son, it wouldn't surprise me if God uses you in days to come to teach the Bible, since you are really good at telling stories." Or, "You have a spirit of adventure about you. It wouldn't surprise me if you end up being a missionary." I believe it is imperative for parents, and even grandparents, to regularly dispense blessings over their children and grandchildren. If you have faith in your kids and believe that they are special and will be used by God in mighty ways, it will directly affect the words you speak over them and the actions you take for them. We see this in the story of Moses. In Hebrews 11, Moses' parents are inducted into what many call the Hall of Faith for protecting him from Pharaoh's decree to kill all the Jewish boys.

> By faith Moses' parents hid him for three months after he was
> born, because they saw he was no ordinary child, and they were
> not afraid of the king's edict.
>
> Hebrews 11:23

I believe that it was through the eyes of faith and trust in God that Jochebed and Amram said of their son Moses, "This child is going to be special" (see Exodus 2:2). They had faith that he would grow up to be no ordinary man. And they had faith to release him into the water and trust God that He would take care of him.

Mom and Dad, if you think your child will never amount to much, that he or she will always struggle or will never be quite up to par—that is simply a lack of faith. In that same chapter in Hebrews, it says that "faith is the substance of things hoped for, the evidence of things not seen" (Hebrews 11:1 KJV). If you see your kid as a problem child, this thought will be understood within their soul, and it will greatly hinder what God can do in and through their life. Declare and believe good things about your child! Be like Jochebed and Amram. Knowing, believing, and having faith that their child would be special, they went to great lengths to make sure his life was spared.

Insights from Sarah

Something my parents consistently did that affected me in tremendous ways was to speak words of life and future direction over my life and my brother's life. Starting when we were young, they would observe our strengths and weaknesses, our natural inclination to hobbies, or our fascination with certain things, and they would use that opportunity to build us up with words of life and vision. For example, they would see that my brother loved playing with Legos and would say, "You are so good at problem-solving and building things, son. You could be an amazing engineer if you wanted to be. The sky's the limit!" Or they would observe the creative side in me and how I loved to read books and tell stories, and they would say, "You could be an entrepreneur or a writer, Sarah!" The funny thing is, those things my parents spoke over our lives actually ended up being what my brother and I became! Crazy, huh?! Now, by no means were we pressured to do anything by our parents; they simply saw our passions at an early age and encouraged us with that "the sky's the limit" kind of thinking. Their confidence and faith in us gave us the confidence and faith in ourselves to walk in whatever the Lord had in store for us. So parents, believe and have faith that your kids have great potential. All kids have an intuitive sense of what their parents believe and think about them. Your faith in them can be the driving force to unlock their greatness.

The Final Blessing

We've touched on a few components of passing on a biblical blessing to your children, and we want to conclude this chapter by adding a final way in which you can be a blessing to your loved ones.

Proverbs 5:18 (NKJV) says, "Let your fountain be blessed." The fountain is symbolic of the family that flows from you. Maybe as you read this, your family isn't all you wish it were. Take heart. No matter how dismal your situation may appear, there's hope, because the Lord has given guidelines for strengthening your relationships with your loved ones.

Deuteronomy 6:5–7 is God's foundation for a strong family: "Love the LORD your God with all your heart and with all your soul and with all your strength. These commandments that I give you today are to be on your hearts. Impress them on your children."

When your relationship with Him is your top priority, you'll affect not only those around you but also future generations. That is how your fountain will be blessed. Say this blessing regularly over your children.

> The LORD bless you and keep you;
> the LORD make his face shine on you and be gracious
> to you;
> the LORD turn his face toward you and give you peace.
>
> Numbers 6:24–26

PUT IT INTO PRACTICE:
APPLYING BIBLICAL BLESSINGS

- Tender Meaningful Touch: Look for ways to shower your kids with touch. Hug them constantly, kiss them, tickle them, give them piggyback rides, hold their faces, look them straight in the eyes and tell them you're proud of them.
- Affirmation: Tell your kids each day that you love them. Remind them of who they are in Christ—they are fearfully and wonderfully made, they are a son or daughter of the Most High God, they are smart, creative, kind, and beautiful.
- Future Direction: Tell your kids that they can do anything that they set their minds to. Dream big together. Remind your kids they can do all things through Christ who strengthens them.

PART THREE

THE ROOT OF THE PROBLEM

5

I'M GOING TO TELL MY KIDS . . .

Breaking Generational Strongholds

Sarah Garcia
@sarahmgarcia

Gonna tell my kids this was Wonder Woman

ave you ever heard of that hilarious viral trend called "Gonna tell my kids. . ."? It's where someone takes a photo and compares it to something that looks similar but isn't it at all, for the sake of rewriting history in a comical way. For instance, there's a meme showcasing Baby Yoda that says, "Gonna tell my kids this was Danny DeVito." Or they'll caption a picture of Iron Man with "Gonna tell my kids this was Elon Musk." You gotta love the internet.

When I first saw this viral trend, I thought it was hilarious, but later it got me thinking. "Gonna tell my kids" shows that life isn't just about you; it's about your kids and their children. It's about what we as parents are passing on to them. What needs to be addressed—and is hardly ever talked about in Christian circles—is the issue of *generational strongholds*.

In Christ, we are a new creation, but there are still thought patterns and habits that we've either picked up from our parents or formed on our own through the years. These thought patterns and habits need to be eradicated before we pass them on to our kids. The enemy is a genius strategizer, and he operates by trial and error. If he sees he's gotten to your parents through a certain weakness (like anger or fear), and he sees that he has gotten to you as well, he'll try the same thing with your kids.

A biblical example of this can be found in the genealogies listed in 1 and 2 Kings. If one king was wicked and didn't repent or change, the child who succeeded him ended up becoming just as wicked, if not more so. A generational stronghold is passed down from one generation to another due to rebellion against God. Another biblical example is seen in Genesis, in the lives of Abraham, Sarah, and Isaac, their son. Abraham had a weakness of fear that led to deceit. More than once when he was traveling in a foreign land, he lied and said that Sarah was his sister because he was afraid that the king would kill him and take her (because Sarah was very beautiful). A few chapters later we see

Isaac doing the same exact thing with his wife, Rebekah. The generational stronghold of fear and deceit was passed down to Isaac because it wasn't broken and dealt with in Abraham.

If your family line is marked by divorce, poverty, anger, or other ungodly patterns, you're likely under a generational stronghold. The Bible says that these strongholds are intimately tied to our choices. Deuteronomy 30:19 says we can choose either life and blessing or death and cursing. Our families have the greatest influence on our development, including the development of our patterns of sin.

I counseled a girl who was very pessimistic in her thinking. She always looked at the glass as half empty, and it was hard for her to even see the positive in any situation. I asked her questions about her parents, and she said her mom was very pessimistic. This is what I call the shadow side of behavior, passed down through the generations.

Whether it is a multigenerational family stronghold or a pattern of thinking or habit that began with you, God has a plan for your freedom that will shatter the chains of that cycle forever! It will be stopped not only in your life, but also from being passed on to your children and grandchildren.

> The word of the LORD came to me again, saying, "What do you mean when you use this proverb concerning the land of Israel, saying: 'The fathers have eaten sour grapes, and the children's teeth are set on edge'? "As I live," says the Lord GOD, "you shall no longer use this proverb in Israel. Behold, all souls are Mine; the soul of the father as well as the soul of the son is Mine."
>
> Ezekiel 18:1–4 NKJV

This was a popular proverb in ancient Israel at the time (kinda like how today we say, "Oh, this song is my jam," ancient Jews were saying, "Oh, this proverb is my jam"). They had the mentality that their problems were not their fault—it was because of the sins of their ancestors. Some people today point to Deuteronomy 5:9, which says that God is a jealous God who visits the iniquity of the fathers to the third and fourth generation, and believe that verse means a family can have a "generational curse." God makes it very clear in Ezekiel 18:3 that this proverb shouldn't be used anymore because He deals with people individually. The warning in Deuteronomy 5:9 is to those who continue in the wicked pattern of their fathers. The very next verse, 10, states God's blessings are poured out abundantly on those who love and obey Him. Clearly each person answers to God individually, making a choice to accept the righteousness that God provides or to reject Him and live in sin.

There is a difference, however, between a *generational curse* and a *generational stronghold*. Another way to explain a generational stronghold is a proclivity to a certain sin like pride, jealousy, or pornography. Dr. Caroline Leaf, in her book *Switch on Your Brain*, explains it like this: A generational stronghold is a biological response to an environmental signal that can be inherited through the generations. These responses can be in the form of depression, addiction, anger, et cetera. But if you remove the environmental signal, the responses fade. If you *introduce* a signal, however—for example, saying something like, "My mom had depression, and now I have depression, so my daughter will have depression"—then those responses are activated. "Thinking and speaking out the problem serves as the signal that makes it a reality," Dr. Leaf wrote. The reverse is true, if we say that "those chains are broken, I will not have depression," then the signals are removed as well as the responses. They can be broken.[1]

John 8:31–36 reminds us that as we abide in Jesus Christ, we receive His freedom. Not only has Jesus redeemed us from our sins, but He has also set us free from the penalty, the moral liability, and the ongoing curse of that sin! It doesn't have to be "like father, like son." This redemption comes as we understand that the root of our problems is in the spiritual realm. Jesus Christ is the Anointed One. That means He is the burden-removing, yoke-destroying Power of God in our lives. As we apply God's Word to our lives, and we choose to walk in righteousness and obedience to God, the chains of bondage will be broken. The fathers may eat sour grapes, but the children's teeth will not be set on edge; the pattern is broken. Through the shed blood of Jesus Christ, we have a new and better covenant with God the Father. He forgives us our sin and delivers us from iniquity. He transforms our hearts and renews our minds. The freedom we have longed for can become a reality!

The Brain Can Change

Applying the Word even has the ability to reshape our brains. Did you know that thoughts are real-life substances that can change the way our brains operate? We see Bible verses about renewing the mind, taking thoughts captive, and as you think so you are. All these verses predicted what modern neuroscience is now discovering—that *your brain can change through your thoughts*. Genetic determinism says that you inherit 50 percent of your DNA spiral ladder from your mom and the other 50 percent of your genome from your dad, making you a set-in-stone by-product of them. Basically, in layman's terms, what this is saying is that you are the way you are because of your parents and nothing can change that. Well, now modern science is discovering that is not the case.

Daniel Amen was a psychiatrist who did 83,000 brain scans over his twenty-two-year career—that's more brain scans than anyone in history (I know, *mind blowing*, right?). The single most important discovery he and his colleagues made was that the brain can change.[2] How does this happen? Through our thoughts! Once you take your thoughts captive (see 2 Corinthians 10:5) and start meditating on and declaring the truth of God's Word over your life, your neural pathways can redirect from negative thought patterns to positive thought patterns, thus changing the way your brain operates.

If you're reading this and you know that there are thought patterns (strongholds) that you've struggled with, and your parents struggled with, and you do not want to showcase to your children—there's hope! Start each day with daily declarations saturated in God's Word. Meditate on these declarations and declare them out loud over yourself. Start to think and meditate on things that are true. It's a process, but over time your neural pathways will redirect and you'll find yourself not always thinking thoughts of fear, but of hope and faith. Your knee-jerk reaction won't be anger but self-control. The Holy Spirit will help you along in this journey through prayer.

You don't have to be stuck in a rut anymore. You don't have to leave a crack open in the door of your mind for the enemy to continue to work. You can choose to have the buck stop with you and declare that instead of generational strongholds, your children and your children's children will have generational freedom. Hallelujah!

Insights from Sarah

There has been a generational stronghold of fear on both of my parents' sides throughout a good portion of my life. I wrestled with it too, until I'd had enough. Whenever fear would come, I would replace it with faith and God's perfect love. I would declare Jesus' blood over my life and break off that generational stronghold. The narrative is changing. Someday I'm going to tell my kids that I got rid of the stronghold of fear once and for all so that they don't have to deal with it. I'm going to tell them that I kicked habitual sins to the curb so that they don't have to struggle with them. If you don't think doing it for yourself is enough, then do it for your kids and your kids' kids. Break down generational strongholds and release generational promises!

Copy and Paste

The things that transfer to our kids include not only our appearance, but our character, heart attitudes, ideas, thoughts, love, integrity, and choices as well. Some parents never put away childish things, and it ends up wreaking havoc on their families. The children grow up, and no matter how much they say that they'll never be like their dad or mom, they knowingly or unknowingly follow in their footsteps. The childish ways of their mothers and fathers get "copied and pasted" into them, and from them they are copied and pasted into their children, and on and on the generational cycle continues. This is the root cause, but what is the solution? The solution to this generational cycle is through a little thing called *forgiveness*.

You might want to get your highlighter out for this goodie: *What you don't forgive, you repeat.* That's a fact. No matter how hard it might be, we need to forgive our fathers and mothers, for our children's sake. Like I shared earlier, my father had a drinking problem. He drank because he wanted to numb the fear that he experienced growing up with *his* alcoholic dad. I never fully realized how much his drinking problem had affected me until fear took its toll. I began to experience anxiety and grind my teeth at night. All of these things were surfacing because I never fully forgave my father. Around my thirties, I finally made the decision to forgive him, and through that, the Holy Spirit was able to begin the healing work in my heart and mind. Forgiveness wasn't a single event; rather, it was a daily surrender.

We all bring so much baggage (hurts, wounds, emotional scars, unforgiveness) into our marriages and into parenting. Frank and I were married five years before we were able to have kids, and I thank the Lord for that now. I know He was giving us time to work things out and receive healing before our wonderful children came. As parents, we have to make sure that we continually go to the Lord in prayer and ask the Holy Spirit to excavate those walls and broken things in our hearts.

The Lord wants us to forgive so that healing can begin in our hearts, and so we can be used to our full capacity and potential. He also doesn't want us to "copy and paste" those generational cycles or wounds into our children. Any bitterness or resentment or anger or fear that we might be harboring or holding on to will be passed on if we do not get rid of it. The first step toward this is forgiveness.

Forgiveness is practically impossible apart from the cross. The cross is what gives us the power to forgive those who have hurt us, especially our parents. You might say, "It's not fair. They have to pay for what they did to me," or "They have to pay for what they did to my family." Jesus already paid for what they did to you—on the cross of Calvary. He died not only for your sin, but for their sin. It's done and paid for. By the same measure that you have been graciously forgiven, so too must you forgive. Forgive, and you will be forgiven (see Luke 6:37).

The first step toward healing is obedience to God's Word to forgive. If we don't forgive, we are in danger of being out of the will of God, in danger of hurting ourselves and future generations by keeping that stronghold in place (see Matthew 6:14–15).

The second step is transformation. Romans 12:1–2 says that the key to transformation is renewing the mind. Just like we read earlier in this chapter, the brain can change, but it can happen only through renewing the mind. This is why we need to get real with ourselves and ask the Holy Spirit to reveal those hidden places in our hearts and minds that need to be renewed and transformed. Surround yourself with community and mentors who will help you work through those wounds together. Get counseling. The enemy likes to keep things hidden, he likes to keep us distracted and unaware of our wounds, hearts, and minds so that he can continue devastating for generations. Make this your declaration, parents: "I will forgive, and I will be transformed in my heart and my mind—for myself and my children's sake and their children's sake."

Let's make it our aim to start a whole new copy-and-paste generational cycle—one that looks a lot less like our forefathers and a lot more like our heavenly Father.

Insights from Frank

I'm amazed to see how godly my son and daughter grew up to become, knowing that both my wife and I came from broken households. We were by no means perfect parents—especially me. I found myself apologizing to the family very often. It is by God's grace alone that He gave us the wisdom from His Word and counsel from the Holy Spirit in order to raise our children. But there was another critical thing my wife and I learned. Highlight and underline this next sentence: We learned to humbly repent and ask our kids for forgiveness when we messed up. This is a game-changer because it not only models to your kids humility and repentance, but it shows your kids that you don't have it all together and we are all in need of God's grace. Apologizing to your kids when you mess up will unite your family more than any other thing.

Insights from Sarah

When I was growing up, my parents did occasionally get in arguments with each other, but the beautiful thing to see was that if they ever argued in front of us, they made sure to make up in front of us. They would tell us, "We're sorry that we yelled in frustration." They didn't shift the blame but simply owned up to it and said they were wrong. Turns out, humility and asking for forgiveness is very contagious. My brother and I saw them exemplify that so well that it made it easy for us to walk in humility, repent fully, and ask for forgiveness from each other. We saw in their example that when you own up to something, it no longer owns you. They didn't have to sit us down and command us to say sorry to each other—we simply saw how freeing it was to them when they asked for forgiveness from us, and we were more than willing to do the same.

Trip Wire Warning

In the movie *Behind Enemy Lines*, actor Owen Wilson plays a US Navy pilot who gets shot down behind enemy lines. The enemy, wanting to take him out for recording their secret armory, sends two military men (one a captain and one a sniper) to hunt Owen Wilson's character down. Those two military men are rivals, and while they are walking through the forest, the sniper, wanting to eliminate his competition, sees a trip wire and quietly steps over it, leaving the captain to step right on top of it and die. Suspenseful, I know. That scene makes for a good movie-watching experience, but when the sniper's actions are unintentionally applied to parenting and generational strongholds, it can amount to destruction.

The trip wire is symbolic of all the traumatic things we've gone through in our lives. It's the secret sins we hid for so long.

It's the personal failures and wrong heart attitudes like pride and jealousy. To protect our kids from stepping on the same trip wire that caused us to stumble, we need to be willing to go there with them. If you never teach them about these things, they'll walk right into the same traps that you did. The enemy is smart. If he sees that he was able to get to you and your family tree with certain temptations, he'll do it with your kids. This is why it is crucial to set aside times when you can talk about your weaknesses and all the difficult things you struggled with in your past and your spouse's past. Draw up a family tree and write some of the things that you have observed in your life and in your extended family that the enemy has used to get a foothold. If there's pornography, write that down. If there's lying, stealing, greed, addictions, sibling rivalry, gender confusion, victimhood, pride, anger, fear, write it all down.

Becoming aware of it and making your kids aware of it is the first and most crucial step. This will keep you on guard against the enemy's sneaky temptations and attacks. But don't leave it at that. Here's the most important thing you can do: Tell your kids where God has been good and what Jesus has done in your life. Tell them that God can take your family tree and weave it through a different tree, a tree called Calvary. Tell them that Jesus can cancel any generational strongholds and negative proclivities and He can write a new story. That new story can be a legacy of faith and righteousness. Tell your kids that those demons and temptations have no power over them, and that the enemy's power has been broken and overcome through the blood of Jesus and the word of their testimony! This is how you can effectively warn your kids about the trip wire.

Parents, we've been given the authority through the blood of Jesus to break down any generational stronghold in our lives. Therefore, let's ask the Holy Spirit to show us anything in our hearts or minds that needs to be transformed and renewed. We need to let go of anger, unforgiveness, and even negative thinking. Confess habitual, secret sin. Don't leave a crack open in your family's door that the enemy can sneak into. This is the spiritual side of parenting that never gets talked about, but I wanted to emphasize it because all my life, I've seen strongholds at work in my extended family members. My husband and I have experienced it in our own lives too. I'm here to tell you that we need to beat the enemy to the punch. Strip off anything that will hinder your kids. It will be a process, especially when it comes to patterns of thinking and fear, but the Holy Spirit living inside of you will help you overcome it.

Next, after we've worked on ourselves, we need to make our children aware of the enemy's tactics. They need to know that the things they do and how they think will not only affect them but their own children and their children's children. A lie that most kids believe is that their attitudes and sin don't affect anyone, but in fact, they do. Awareness of generational strongholds is the first step, and the second step is teaching our kids how to overcome them.

Fear and pride were generational strongholds that had their run in both sides of my family and my husband's. Once I started to see my daughter struggle with it at an early age, we knew we had to teach her how to overcome it and cut it off. This was a turning point for me when I saw my daughter echo our strongholds. That's when I realized that she was dealing with the things that I had not faced off with. I believe our children will inherit one of two things: either God's promises or our strongholds. If we don't deal with those things, then we leave our children to deal with them. And guess what? Those strongholds get stronger with every generation. We don't have the right to remain comfortable or captive when other people need us to be free. This is the key to the entirety of this book: *Become the person that you want to see your children grow up to be.*

Shoot with the Bow

Shooting with the bow is a phrase in the Bible used to illustrate the prophetic. Second Kings 13:14–16 depicts this perfectly with the story of Elisha's last prophecy. Most Christian parents don't know how to shoot arrows and prophesy. Prophesying is simply taking a word that God gives you today and shooting it into tomorrow. What does this look like? If your children are backslidden, you shoot an arrow by declaring that all your children will come back to the Lord. You shoot and declare that greater is He that is in them than he that is in the world (see 1 John 4:4). You shoot into your family's future and declare that all your children shall grow up in the house of God. That they will be princes or princesses of the Most High. Shoot the Word of God into their future. We're in a time right now when the enemy is running rampant trying to steal the hearts of your children with the temptations of the world. Everything in culture is pointing them away from Christ and the truth of the Word to the ways of the world. Now more than ever, parents must use everything in their arsenal to fight for their children. This includes shooting arrows.

Turn it around to yourself and begin to declare that every generational stronghold is broken off of your life. Declare that your children are a stronghold-breaking generation. Declare that your children shall not grow up with the same dysfunction, the same disabilities that you had to face. Determine that you're going to take down these giants in your life so that your children can walk to heights that you never were able to. Shoot into your tomorrow. Shoot into their tomorrow. Prophesy in faith.

Let's be families that declare, "I'm going to tell my kids that I am a new creation in Christ, and I have conquered and put off those areas in my life where the enemy once had a stronghold— we are free!"

Pray against the generational strongholds over you and your family—anything that you might have inherited from generations before. The enemy has been using the same weapon on your grandfather or grandmother that he uses on you—stop holding back and shying away from the fight against insecurity. It's time to pick up the right weapons! It stops with you and your family. The strongholds that have come after your family line, they stop today. The enemy will try to get you to focus on the surface-level things, but start with your heart—are there people you need to forgive? Today, you pick up the shield of faith. Today, you pick up the sword of the Spirit.

Pray This over Yourself:

Holy Spirit, I thank You that Your power is coming into my home right now. I speak against every spirit that has come against generations. Right now, I break every chain in the name of Jesus! Lord, I thank You that_____ and any other sin is broken in the name of Jesus! Fear and anxiety that have plagued families is broken in the name of Jesus! Thank You that my family is free now in Jesus' name!

Daily Declaration:

My new bloodline is stronger than my old one. My new DNA in Christ is *greater* than my old one in Adam. I am the *stronghold breaker*! I am the one who will break and destroy every generational stronghold that has ever controlled and oppressed my family! I am the one unlocking and releasing *generational blessings* into my life and family! Right now, God is severing all unhealthy attachments and ties to me. He is setting the record straight over my home. The generational dysfunctions I grew up in are no longer mine to continue in. This is the season when God begins a new thing in my home.

PUT IT INTO PRACTICE:
STEPS TO BREAK GENERATIONAL STRONGHOLDS

- Get alone with God and ask Him if there's any unforgiveness, bitterness, or hurt that you're holding in your heart toward someone, and ask God to help you forgive that person.
- Ask the Holy Spirit to reveal any generational strongholds or proclivities in your life (pride, jealousy, gossip, fear, pessimism). Say the declaration above over that stronghold and start to replace it daily with the Word of God. This is how you'll renew your mind.
- Look to the cross and remember how much Jesus has forgiven you. When we look to the cross, we are able to forgive with the help of the Holy Spirit. Remember, that which you don't forgive, you repeat. Don't repeat the same things that were done to you. Forgiveness breaks the cycle. And it gives you a new copy-and-paste mode—the heart of Jesus.

6

THE HEART OF THE PROBLEM

Parenting the Heart

Insights from Sarah

I remember my first day of college. I was nervous and excited at the same time. I had just moved into my dorm, met my roommate, and headed out to my very first class. I picked a seat in the front of the stadium room, sat down, pulled out my laptop, and was ready to soak up the lecture. My professor surprised us by starting off the class with an announcement I'll never forget because it went against how I thought school should be. He stated that he was *not* going to be taking attendance all semester. He told us that we were adults now and needed to be treated like adults. Adulthood comes with the responsibility of showing up to class. He bluntly said that if we wanted to ditch class and throw away hundreds of dollars, then that would be on us. If we actually came to college to learn, however, then we would make it a priority to be at every class. He left the decision up to us and, to be honest, it shocked us all. We weren't being forced to follow the rules anymore; it had to come from our own desire to want to come to class and learn. That pivotal decision to move from following rules to heart conviction changed the trajectory of that class and shaped my entire college experience.

I n the classic Christmas movie *How the Grinch Stole Christmas*, we see that the Grinch had a heart problem. No, he didn't suffer physically, but emotionally. There were deep hurts, wounds, and hatred that had built up in his heart. As the Grinch grew up, those wounds to his heart caused it to become small and hardened. He hated Christmas the most because it reminded him of everything that he didn't have: family, love, and laughter. The Grinch stole all of the presents from every household in Whoville, hoping that would ruin Christmas. It ended up backfiring on the Grinch when all of Whoville came together in song and in love. They knew Christmas was not about presents but about presence with those they loved. That touching moment caused the Grinch to finally break down and cry out, "Help me—I'm feeling!" Then, it's said, the Grinch's small heart grew three sizes that day. His heart transformation led the Grinch to become an entirely different person. This movie points out the place from which all of our problems stem—the heart.

At the heart of every problem is a problem of the heart.

The heart is the core of our being, and the Bible sets high importance on keeping our hearts pure: "Above all else, guard your heart, for everything you do flows from it" (Proverbs 4:23). According to Scripture, the biggest problem humanity has is the heart.

Our heart includes our desires, emotions, morality, and motivations, and it's where sin ultimately takes root. Parenting needs to be centered on the heart and not on behavior. If God is concerned about heart transformation over behavior modification, then we as parents need to be too. Growing up, my parents did the best they knew how to parent us, but when I got married, my husband and I had to look to the Word to find out how our heavenly Father parents His children. Over and over again, we saw that the Lord cares about our hearts—the motivation behind our behaviors. It's easy for parents to fall into the trap of merely focusing on their child's behavior. Behavior is what we can see, so it tends to be what we respond to most. While focusing on behavior might be effective in the short term, we need to dig deeper if we want to have an impact on our children's spiritual development. Let's start digging with the best tool available: God's Word.

Bible Story Time: God Cares about Our Hearts

In 1 Samuel 15, God gives Saul a clear instruction through the prophet Samuel: Wage war against the Amalekites and completely destroy them and their belongings as punishment for their wickedness against His people. Saul goes out, fights, wins the war, and brings back the king of the Amalekites and the best of the plunder. God pronounces a judgment on Saul, stating that his kingdom will be removed from him because of his lack of complete obedience. To paraphrase, Saul replies, "But God, I saved all the good stuff for *You*!" God's answer is not what Saul expects. God replies that "to obey is better than sacrifice" (verse 22).

What we see from this story is that God didn't want the sacrifices that Saul offered to Him. He didn't care for the burnt offerings of the plunder—God wanted Saul's heart. God cares about our hearts: the intent behind our behavior. Saul put his interest over God's because his heart was proud and greedy. He wanted to parade his victory rather than obey God by annihilating the Amalekites completely. We find out that later down the road, Saul's lack of complete obedience comes back to bite the Jewish people in the book of Esther, when Haman almost wipes out the Jews. Because guess whose Haman's ancestors were? The Amalekites. This goes to show that your heart not only affects you, but it affects your descendants for generations to come.

Ultimately, we are judged not because of our behavior, but because of what our behavior reveals about our hearts. Behavior is much easier to see, so it is much easier to discipline. If we see our kids having a tantrum in the middle of the grocery store because they can't get their favorite sugary cereal, it's much easier to focus our attention on their tantrum than to see what the real heart problem is behind the tantrum.

So now we get down to the nitty-gritty—how do we "parent the heart"? One of the most effective tools that you and I have available to affect the hearts of our children is not a cookie-cutter method or strategy. It's not about creating a pie chart or a reward system with stars and demerits. But rather, it's about focusing on our *own* heart. As we already know, *kids mirror parents*. It is especially true for issues of the heart. That's why it's so important that we, as parents, first focus on getting our hearts right before parenting our children's hearts. This is not to guarantee, however, that your kids will have good hearts. Adam still rebelled against God even though he had the perfect parent—God Himself. But you can rest assured that your godly example and the Word of God that is planted in them will not return void. Even if it takes time.

Just as Saul's army did not obey the Lord's command because Saul's own heart was not devoted to God, we cannot expect to lead our children in the ways of God if our own hearts are not seeking after the Lord. Through the power of the Holy Spirit and prayer, we need to continually assess the condition of our own hearts. We need to evaluate our motivation for doing what we do. We need to live our faith out loud right in front of our kids—not a religious, white-washed faith, but one that is "worked out with fear and trembling" amid the ups and downs of life. We need to come before the Lord in prayer, and like David in Psalm 139:23–24, ask the Lord to search our hearts. Remember, the greatest thing you can do is love the Lord with all your heart, mind, and strength. In other words, be who you want your children to be.

Parenting the Hearts of Your Children

Have you been facing many challenges as a parent and are wondering where you're going wrong? Remember that behavior is just the result of a *spiritual heart condition*, and we must dig into the source to make a deeper impact. I have a master's degree in counseling ministry, and throughout all my counseling sessions, I have come to realize that it is far easier to shape a child than to repair an adult. Get to the heart issues of your kids while they are still in your care. Rooting out wrong heart attitudes and issues before they become young adults is much easier because their hearts haven't had years to grow and harden. We often think that once we are saved, our hearts become perfectly pure—rid of any dirt. Though the blood of Jesus has fully redeemed us and given us a new spirit, our hearts and minds are the last bastions of rebellion. They need to be transformed and renewed, as Romans 12:1–2 instructs.

Insights from Sarah

If I had a tissue for every heart issue that I struggled with in my life, I would definitely have a whole Kleenex box. Since this book is HOT (Humble, Open, and Transparent), I want to share one of my own heart issues in hopes of opening your eyes to its hidden and detrimental repercussions. One of my heart issues was pride. Pride showed itself in my life by never wanting to say sorry, getting defensive if someone corrected me or told me I was wrong, undermining authority, taking credit for something that wasn't mine, or bragging about my accomplishments. The result, at least in my life, eventually bubbled up into anxiety. Pride made me think I could control everything when, deep down, I knew I couldn't, which led to anxiety. I had to go through a hard trial in my life to finally surrender and let the Lord do complete heart surgery on me to rid me of pride.

I wish I would have paid more attention to the root cause behind my behaviors growing up. My parents brought it up, but it never fully clicked until I was a young adult that my behaviors were driven by my heart. Becoming aware of those heart issues, repenting from them, and asking the Holy Spirit to transform my heart would have saved me a whole lot of pain and suffering in my life.

What I've come to find in my life is that the deeper I grow in my intimacy with Jesus, the more He starts to reveal those heart issues and transform me from the inside out. It takes a surrendered, "die to yourself" mentality to start the work of heart surgery. The Bible refers to it as being clay in the Potter's hand. We are the clay, and we have to be willing to surrender ourselves to the Potter's hands to allow Him to shape and mold us back into the way He intended us to be. I took a pottery class in high school, and boy, let me tell you, it is a very messy process, but the reward is so worth it.

If you didn't know, my family and I are from Southern California, and "we Californians" are definitely known for our love of all things organic and gluten-free. I hate to admit it, but some churches here not only serve gluten-free Communion wafers, but gluten-free, keto-friendly, USDA organic, chia seed Communion wafers! Another thing that has become very popular on the West Coast is functional medicine. Functional medicine is a systems and biology-based approach to medicine that focuses on identifying and addressing the root cause of disease. Medical doctors often prescribe countless pharmaceutical medications to treat your symptoms, instead of getting to the root of those symptoms and bringing healing to that area naturally (e.g., eliminating inflammatory foods and eating healthy, detoxing, taking herbs and natural supplements, getting enough sunlight, etc.). I have struggled through the years with symptoms of joint pain and inflammation. I only made headway in it after I started treating the root of the problem. Getting to the root of the problem is the only way toward lasting healing and transformation. The same is true with parenting. According to Luke 6:45, what your children say and do is a reflection of what is in their hearts (the root):

A good man brings good things out of the good stored up in his heart, and an evil man brings evil things out of the evil stored up in his heart. For the mouth speaks what the heart is full of.

Over and over again the Bible focuses on the heart, and so should we in parenting. Just like when a car breaks down, we don't try to fix the exterior, we go straight to the heart of the car—the engine. That's the source that drives the car.

Parenting is determined by the heart, yet parents often get sidetracked with behavior because it's what alerts you to your child's need for discipline. Behavior, like throwing tantrums in the grocery store, is very irritating and calls attention to itself. You think you have corrected the behavior by saying, "Stop crying! Stop being disrespectful! That's wrong!" But the symptom keeps rearing its head over and over again because you didn't get to the root. Behavior does not just spring forth uncaused. So if we, as their loving parents, want to really help them, we must be concerned with the heart attitudes that drive their behavior.

If you're wondering what type of heart problems to look for, here are some examples that indicate heart attitudes gone wrong:

Envy: Being jealous of siblings and the resulting conflict.

Strife: Having problems of any kind with their siblings.

Deceit: Being less than honest about what they have said or done.

Gossip: Talking negatively about someone to someone else.

Insolence: Being rude and unmannerly.

Haughtiness: Pride—not taking correction, not wanting to apologize, taking credit for other people's work, not coming under authority.

Boastfulness: Declaring that they are better, smarter, prettier, faster, stronger, et cetera, than others.

Foolishness: Not acting in God's wisdom; conceited.

Heartlessness: Not caring about others, only themselves.

A change in behavior that does not come from a changed heart will always mean the symptoms will keep coming back again. An excellent example of this is the Pharisees that Jesus condemned. In Matthew 15, Jesus rebukes the Pharisees who honor God with their lips, but whose hearts are far from Him. In Matthew 23, He even compares them to a white-washed tomb that looks good on the outside, but the inside is filled with dead men's bones. This is exactly the detriment of most parenting—demanding a nice, polished-white behavior on the outside, but never bringing to light the decaying bones on the inside.

You might be thinking now, *Okay, okay, I get it. Don't parent behavior, parent the heart. But how in the blue blazes do I do that?* As parents, we must require proper behavior, don't get me wrong, but we can never just leave it at that. The key is to *understand*—and help our children understand—how their heart condition has resulted in wrong behavior.

Let's Get Real

Let's take an everyday example from when my twins were young. Let's say Sal and Sarah are playing, and all of a sudden a fight breaks out over a toy. I could scurry on over and give a classic response like, "Okay, who had it first?" But this would completely miss the heart of the problem. In fact, it actually turns it into a justice issue that favors the child who had the quickest draw to pick up the toy first. And if we know the justice system at all, we know that going down that road leads to even more problems. Looking at this situation in terms of the heart, both Sal and Sarah are wrong. They are both displaying the heart attitude of selfishness. Sal and Sarah are both effectively say-ing, "I only care about myself, and do not get in my way." (Cue Violet from *Charlie and the Chocolate Factory*, "But Daddy, I want a pony and I want it now!")

When you put your heart-issue glasses on, you'll see that I have not one but two children at fault. Two children are being selfish. One might have taken it away from the other, but the other still wants it back, which means the heart issue is the same: "I want my happiness, even at your expense."

At the heart of every problem is a problem of the heart. This perspective and understanding will positively affect how you discipline because it is about more than just changed behavior. Instead of walking up to my children and saying, "Who had it first?" or "You two better stop fighting and share!" I would walk up to them and confront what is occurring in their hearts. I would *reveal their wrong heart attitudes* and help them under-stand how it reflects a heart that has strayed. I would say, "Sal and Sarah, what you are doing is showing a heart that is selfish and only cares for itself. Jesus tells us that we are to put others' needs above our own. When we do that, we feel happier than when we are being selfish." And while we're helping unmask their heart issues, we must always point to the cross. We need to help our children understand sin and their need for a Savior.

I have a little doggie named Faith. Faith is a Maltipoo (Mal-tese/mini poodle), and she looks like a little white lamb. Little Faith follows me everywhere I go around the house. She's like my little lamb, which is quite funny since my name is Mary (like in the children's nursery rhyme). She follows me every-where, and it reminds me that I am a shepherd, not only to her, but most importantly, to my children. As parents, we need to learn how to shepherd our children's hearts. We must learn to see behavior and ask the Holy Spirit to show us the underlying heart condition. Your child's heart has a natural tendency to bend away from God, and your job is to bend it back toward God, parenting the heart with discipline and love.[1]

Here are some practical applications to shepherd the heart of a child.

1. When a problem occurs, engage them; don't merely correct their behavior. You must help them become aware and see the root of their behavior.

2. Pray for your kids that the Lord would remove any heart of stone (bad heart attitudes) and put in them a heart of flesh (Ezekiel 36:26). And also let your kids pray for themselves. Awareness of their heart condition is the first step to heart change.

3. After awareness comes a willingness to surrender. Help them see their need for a Savior and a transformed heart. But that willingness won't come until their relationship with the Lord is deepened. *Love* always leads to change. That's why it's so important to take your kids back to the cross continually. A realization of who Jesus is and what He did for you makes you fall deeper in love with Him. Take Communion regularly with them. Communion is the way that we remember the sacrifice Jesus made for us at the cross. It will be explained in more detail in the next chapter.

4. Appeal to your kids on a heart level, which is the wisdom level. Take them through Proverbs, particularly chapters 3 and 4. Show them the wisdom behind the proverbs and why they don't want to follow after folly but wisdom. Most of the proverbs are guidance for the young and describe the long-term consequences for following wisdom or following folly. Train your kids to be long-term oriented or prudent. Train that into their

thinking. Show them that our decisions won't just affect us four years down the road, but forty.

Let's Get Even More Real

As parents, we need to constantly ask the Holy Spirit to reveal those underlying heart conditions in our children's behaviors. The earlier you start teaching morals and virtues, the better. Just like languages are learned best when children are very young, so are morality, character, and self-control. Here are some examples of practical application for parenting the heart.

In everyday home life, make it your aim to reveal to your kids their heart attitudes that are being repeated, either knowingly or unknowingly. For example, "Samantha, you've been putting your brother down a lot, especially when he excels in something. Ask God to see if there's any pride or jealousy in your heart." Or: "Luke, I've noticed selfishness is becoming an idol in your heart. Let's work on that today. Please serve everyone's dinner plate to them before serving yourself."

Speak in language around your children that will call out sin in their hearts. Awareness is the first step to real, lasting heart change. Talking to your kids on a heart level will make them see that you care about their hearts and want their hearts right with God.

Model to your kids what it's like to have a kind heart, and teach them how to do it. For example, stop and give a homeless person money and have your kids say a quick prayer over them. Or ask your kids if they have noticed anyone who is wearing the same clothes day after day at school. Ask them if they would use their allowance money to buy that person new clothes and shoes as a gesture of kindness.

Explain to your kids that the power of death and life are in the tongue (see Proverbs 18:21) and have them deliberately train their hearts by speaking words of life over their siblings. Go around the dinner table and have your children say what they love most about the person sitting to their right.

Be in God's Word together. Hebrews 4:12 says, "For the word of God is alive and active. Sharper than any double-edged sword, it penetrates even to dividing soul and spirit, joints and marrow; it judges the thoughts and attitudes of the heart." God's Word is like a self-reflecting sword. It allows us to see how we really look on the inside and convicts and reveals things that we might have been unaware of.

With this in mind, we have to remember that God never likes to be put in a box. He works in mysterious ways and deals with people differently. That's why I could never offer you a clear methodology or "10 Steps to Raising Trouble-Free Children." Rather, I can explore with you ways in which *you* can creatively shepherd your children's hearts. My deepest desire is to help you and your kids walk in all the Lord has for you. Dealing with the heart early on is like getting an "Advance to Go" card in Monopoly. You skip all those hotels and payments and pass directly to "Go" (and get your $200 cash).

Our heavenly Father is a good Father to us, and like all good fathers, He sometimes allows trials and pain in our lives to get our hearts right. He sees, in His foreknowledge, that our current heart condition will lead us down a destructive path and keep us from our calling, so He allows trials to deepen our walk with Him, stretch our faith, and wake us up to the fact that our hearts need to change. I had to go through much pain and trial because I was either not aware of my heart issues or stubborn enough to not want to change. That's why, as parents, we need to make sure we are working on addressing those heart issues in our children's hearts early on so they won't have to go through so much pain and suffering down the road. It's much easier to change the heart of a child than that of an adult who is set in their ways.

Insights from Frank

As I look back on raising our son and daughter, one of the toughest things I had to do was continually and constantly be a good example to our children. I did not want to be a hypocrite. As a child, I would be so discouraged when my dad would tell me not to misbehave, not to lie, and when I got older, he would also tell me not to drink. But as I was told all these dos and don'ts, I would see my dad doing the exact opposite. My dad literally drank himself to death at the age of thirty-six, when I was eight years old. As I grew up, I had no idea how to be a good dad or husband or what a good example looked like. By the grace of God, His Word and His Spirit within me gave me the wisdom and the love to strive always to be a good example to them. I was not always perfect, but when I blew it in some way, I would talk to them and sincerely ask for their forgiveness. I have beautiful memories of them saying, "I forgive you, Daddy," and then us moving on joyfully. This is crucial in raising children of godly character. It was not easy, but the fruit I see now in my son's and daughter's lives is all worth it. It is not about just disciplining so your children obey you even when you're not around. The key is to reach their hearts, and their hearts will be molded as they watch you. So when they go off to college, they will choose rightly because you reached their heart. That is the heart of the matter.

I hope this encourages you, dads and moms. No matter what kind of parents you had or what kind of upbringing, there should be no excuse. We have a heavenly Father, His holy Word, and the Holy Spirit to help us be great dads and moms, full of God's wisdom and love.

Endgame: Jesus at Home in Your Heart

When you truly get to know me, you'll find that I'm not your average mom. I like going to rock concerts (Christian rock concerts), and I love watching Marvel movies. One of my favorites was the last Avengers movie called *Endgame*. I mean, you can't get more epic than when Captain America picks up Thor's hammer or when Tony Stark says, "I am Iron Man." Just like *Endgame* perfectly wrapped up an epic saga, there is also an endgame to shepherding your children's hearts. The endgame is to have Jesus at home in their hearts.

When Paul was finishing his letter to the Ephesian church, he said, "For this reason I kneel before the Father, from whom every family in heaven and on earth derives its name. I pray that out of his glorious riches he may strengthen you with power through his Spirit in your inner being, so that Christ may dwell in your hearts through faith" (Ephesians 3:14–17). The word *dwell* means to be at home, so the idea is that Jesus would be at home in your heart. It's almost like inviting Jesus into your home and having Him take off His shoes, get settled and comfortable, and help Himself to the fridge. That should be our prayer for our kids, that Jesus would be at home in their hearts. Not just allowed in peripherally, but that He would settle down deep and be comfortable dwelling there.

How does this happen? Jesus said in Revelation 3:20, "I stand at the door and knock. If anyone hears my voice and opens the door, I will come in." The picture is this: We have to let Jesus come into the home of our heart and let Him into every room, including those dark, spider-webbed closets we never let anyone into. The problem with so many of us is that we make our houses look clean on the surface, but really we just picked up all of our junk and threw it under the bed or into closets. We need to let Jesus into our whole house, let Him spring-clean those areas in our hearts that we've been neglecting. We need to make room in our hearts by ejecting any idols and choosing to put Him on the throne. It might get messy in the process, but the end result is absolutely worth it. This is the analogy we need to keep in mind for our own hearts as parents and for our children's hearts. Make Jesus at home in our hearts.

My vision is to see parents shepherding happy, productive children who are alert to themselves and to life. My heart is to see families that are alive and vibrant—to see teenagers who want to stay at home because home is an exciting and loving place. To see children who highly esteem their parents and constantly go to them for advice. To see biblical truth make its way into every conversation with refreshing ease. To see generations that will keep the faith and make God the foundation for their lives. These are the things worth striving for, and it all starts with the heart. Because, say it with me: At the heart of every problem is a problem of the heart. And we know who sees our hearts, and is the ultimate heart problem solver. "For the LORD does not see as man sees; for man looks at the outward appearance, but the LORD looks at the heart" (1 Samuel 16:7 NKJV).

PUT IT INTO PRACTICE:
PARENTING THE HEART

- Be in constant communication with the Holy Spirit in prayer about your children's hearts. Ask Him to give you wisdom and insight to see what's at the root of their problems.
- Have heart conversations on a constant basis with your children. Make them aware that if they're not obeying or not sharing, it's an issue with their hearts (selfishness, pride).
- Go back to the Let's Get Real section in this chapter and put into practice the tips we offered to help parent your children's hearts.

PART FOUR

FAMILY LIFE

7

THE FAMILY TREE

Family Forms at the Cross

t was a beautiful, sunshiny summer day, and everyone was gearing up for all of the Fourth of July festivities. My family and I had packed up our beloved Winnebago motorhome and had driven to our favorite summer getaway place—Campland, on the Bay in San Diego. We stepped off the motorhome and breathed in that familiar Campland smell—the mix of saltwater and BBQ. There's nothing quite like it. Our first day was filled with Jet Ski rides, soaking up the sun, and hot dogs and hamburgers for dinner. Once the evening started to wind down, we gathered around our kitchen table and pulled out a board game we had just bought at Target the night before. It wasn't a new game, but it was very popular, and none of us had ever played it. We opened up the packaging and there, staring back at us, was an old man with a mustache and top hat, grinning from ear to ear. It was Monopoly. We had heard that this game was great to play with the family because it was a bonding experience. The people that told us that were probably paid off by the Monopoly marketing team, we were soon to discover.

Things started off smoothly. My family was getting the hang of things and buying properties here and there. But the air started to shift ever so slightly as a monopoly was formed and one of my kids landed on it and had to pay the other a whopping amount of money. Negotiations started to take place, and just like that, the competitive nature of the game started to rear its ugly head. Greediness, hurt feelings, bitterness, and just sheer anger started flying out of nowhere. Without warning, our beautiful *Brady Bunch* family suddenly turned into a World War II scene. We had bought this game with the intention that it would knit our family closer together, but it actually drove a wedge between us that we are still trying to get inner healing from to this day. (Okay, that might be a slight exaggeration, but you get the point.) There should be a warning label on the back of the box that reads: WARNING: THIS GAME CONTAINS

CHOKING HAZARDS (AND BY CHOKING HAZARDS WE MEAN PARTY MEMBERS CHOKING EACH OTHER OUT OF SHEER RAGE). PROCEED WITH CAUTION.

The hilarity of it all was that what was supposed to be a fun bonding experience that first night actually did the opposite. We were like bread without the gluten—we just fell apart. The next morning, we decided to bring the spiritual back into our trip and had devotions together. We read the Bible, we played worship songs on our guitars, and we prayed for each other. Afterward, we felt like the gluten was back. We were bonded together once again, and even closer than when we first started the trip. We decided right then and there that family devos, worship, and prayer would be the start of every day for us, especially on vacation. The moral of this story is that although family vacations and game nights can be fun, they won't ever fully bond a family together. Some, like our Monopoly game night, only cause blood pressures to rise. What really bonds a family together—body, soul, and spirit—is the cross of Calvary. *Family forms around the cross.*

John the apostle had a close intimacy with Jesus. He referred to himself as the disciple whom Jesus loved. In his gospel, we read of a very important interaction that occurred between John, Jesus, and Jesus' mother, Mary, while Jesus was hanging on the cross. Here we see the dying words of Jesus at Calvary. He told John to take care of His mother, because they were now family—mother and son (see John 19:25–27). And from that moment, John took Mary into his home. In a moment, the two were bonded together and a family was born. A brand-new family.

Now, you might be thinking, what does this story have to do with parenting? Everything. Get your highlighter out because this is an essential understanding concerning family and the true family tree. We live in a time when there are countless marriage and family books and seminars, with counseling centers full of marriage and family therapists. With all the resources and help, why is the divorce rate still skyrocketing? Why are kids more distant and estranged from their parents than ever before? Why do we see rebellion among teenagers and rejection toward parents when kids grow up? Why do we see the whole thing falling apart at a time when there's an endless number of family books and parenting blogs? Here's the answer: Because people are not factoring in this powerful vignette that happens at the cross. Jesus did more to solve the problem of marriage and family in those two sentences on the cross than all of the *New York Times* bestselling books and counseling clinics have done in decades. It's profoundly simple. The true family tree began when Jesus was on the cross, body convulsing in pain, blood running from His veins. In that moment, a family was born that didn't exist before. In this powerful picture, we see this powerful truth: Family comes together around the cross.

Jesus said to Mary, "Woman, behold thy son." And to John, "Behold thy mother." And that bonding was so powerful that those two stayed together as mother and son without any fracturing or falling apart. The blood of Jesus Christ at the cross caused a bonding to take place that was absolutely unbreakable.

Parents will do anything and everything to try to keep their family together. They'll go on vacations that they can't afford; they'll have family game nights; they'll go on trips to Disneyland thinking Mickey will bond them together. Or how about those family road trips? They think that will for sure bring their family together. How many of you know that not to be so? We thought taking a trip to Campland on the Bay and having a family game night would glue our family together, but it only ended with us getting on each other's nerves. Don't get me wrong, those activities in and of themselves can be good and enjoyed by a family, but we cannot solely rely on them to bond our family together. Hawaii, Monopoly, and road trips won't bond a family together for a lifetime. The bonding takes place at one spot: at the foot of the cross.

Now, one might ask what that looks like. It might include:

- Praying with your spouse every day.
- Having family devotions together on a regular basis—that includes scheduled time and organically talking to your kids about God and the Bible whenever you're around them.
- Having your kids read a proverb of the day when you're driving them to school.
- Asking your kids questions around the dinner table every evening, like "How has God loved you in the last 24 hours?" (This takes the attention off of themselves and other people and puts it onto God.)
- Praying for your kids at bedtime.
- Regularly taking Communion together as a family. Communion is partaking of a small piece of cracker or bread that represents Jesus' body that was broken for us, and drinking juice that represents His blood that was shed for our forgiveness of sins. This is done to remember what Jesus did for us on the cross, and it keeps us walking in repentance, forgiveness, and holiness. Communion should be taken with your kids when they are aware of its meaning and significance. Our kids started at around ten years old.
- Putting on worship music or getting out a guitar and having a worship jam session in the living room together—just like my family did the day after our Monopoly fiasco.

You cannot force your kids to love the Lord, but you can create an environment where they can encounter God and have a fresh revelation of His love toward them. Model to them that worship is not something that we do only when we're at church, but it's a lifestyle of obedience, praise, and glorifying the Lord in all we do.

It's so important that you often take your family to the cross and tell them that the Lord loves them and died for them. By doing that, you show them you care about that. You tell your kids, "Hey, I love you enough to pray for you." "I love you enough to read Proverbs together." "I love you enough to turn on an Elevation Worship song on YouTube and worship Jesus together with you." "And I love you enough to serve Communion and partake together with you." Talk about the lessons He's taught you and the prayers that He's answered. That's so much more important than Monopoly. And your kids will be impacted permanently when they see a mom or dad who takes the time to say, "We're going to seek Jesus together." We also say, "Come to the tree together," because the wooden cross is where Jesus' sacrifice brought us back into relationship with Father God. That is our place of forgiveness, relationship, and worship.

Insights from Sal

My parents knew that our family would have a strong foundation together by gathering at the cross. We took family vacations every so often, but what really bonded us was meeting together every morning before heading off to school and reading a devotional or a chapter from the book of Proverbs together. They would pray for us every single night, no matter how tired they were. We had longer Saturday morning devotionals together, and we would take Communion and pray. In those

Saturday morning devotionals, we would ask each other, "How's your heart?" It allowed us to open up and be real with each other. And the constant communication with my parents brought me closer to them. I could talk to them if something was bothering me, or if something they did hurt me. Gathering at the cross together brought us closer as a family than anything we ever did. Family truly does form at the cross. I'm a real-life testament to that.

I've heard it said so often that families don't have time to gather around the cross because of sports or weekend activities or, here's the kicker, family nights. They don't have time to gather up for devotions because it's family night. Let me tell you something, that's an oxymoron (emphasis on the last five letters of that word). Quality time in and of itself is not the answer. Don't fall for the mentality of, "Well, my kids will be fine if I just make sure I take them to basketball games, make sure we are all together on family vacations, and ensure that we all join in on family nights." In the end, if you don't take them to the place where true bonding happens—at the cross of Calvary—none of it matters. We need to be the parents who pray with our kids, serve Communion to them, and open our hearts to them and say, "This is what the Lord means to me, and I want to share it with you." "We're going to be at church together, kids. In addition to the church being within the four walls of the church building, it can also be here, within our family."

Proverbs 22:6 (KJV) says, "Train up a child in the way he should go: and when he is old, he will not depart from it." This is key. God created these little kids that, when they're younger, they're like sponges—they take in anything you tell them. They don't forget anything. They learn things so quickly, and they adapt even faster. They learn things in such an amazing way that God says whatever it is you want to instruct them in—any routine, any practice, anything you want to instill into their life—start doing it when they are young. So when they grow up, they're so used to it that they're not going to depart from it—that's a promise from God. And that could be small things and big things. Small things can be brushing teeth, cleaning up after yourself, being polite, and using your pleases and thank-yous. Big things can be such things as being wise with money, saving, tithing, showing kindness, respecting elders, showing God's love to people, fearing God, serving at the local church. In my family, Sunday is the Lord's Day. We love to be at church, even when we're on vacation, and wherever we are we visit a local church. Reading God's Word is a big one. When you're having your quiet time with the Lord, when you're on your knees praying, let them see you. *The greatest teacher for your kids is how you live your life.* Let them come sit with you in the morning while you are reading the Word. Our family made it a goal to read the whole Bible together. In each of our private devotions, we would go verse by verse and do an in-depth study of the passage during the week, and then we'd come together on Saturday and discuss our readings together. Instill these healthy traditions and habits now. It's never a guarantee that they'll give their life to the Lord. Salvation is something different for every person. They will have to really seek the Lord and give their heart to God themselves. You cannot do it for them. But boy, you will be setting them onto the right path if you're already instilling in them the importance of reading the Word. And the Word does not come back void. They're going to be used to reading the Word and diving in there, and that could be something God uses to bring them to His feet.

PUT IT INTO PRACTICE:
TAKING YOUR FAMILY TO THE CROSS

- Starting this week, add family bonding activities to your family's schedule.
- Ask your spouse what time of day works best for you to pray together, and be disciplined enough to stick to it.
- Pray together about what God would want you to do for family devotions, and when. Be sure to give your kids a heads-up about it.
- Have your own answer ready, Mom and Dad, when asking, "How has God loved you today?"
- Explain Communion to your children and let them know why you are doing it together as a family.

8

AS FOR ME AND MY HOUSE

Spiritual Leadership and Home Field Advantage

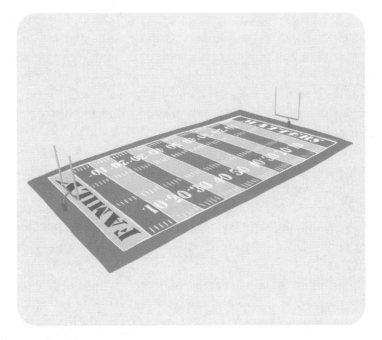

reat historical figures are often remembered for great historical quotes. "Give me liberty or give me death!" Patrick Henry thundered in the days of the American Revolution.[1] "The only thing we have to fear is fear itself," Franklin Roosevelt spoke during the dark days of the Great Depression (very much applicable for the days we are living in now).[2] "Ask not what your country can do for you—ask what you can do for your country," John F. Kennedy said in his first inaugural speech in Washington, D.C.[3] "Never give in, never give in, never, never, never," said a powerful orator, that bulldog of a man, Winston Churchill, as he addressed his alma mater during their graduation ceremony.[4] "One small step for man, one giant leap for mankind" was uttered by the first person to put his foot on the surface of the moon, Neil Armstrong.[5] "No, Luke, I am your father," said Darth Vader to Luke Skywalker (sorry, I had to throw that one in there).

There is a great historical quote in the Bible from a giant of a figure in his day—Joshua. On the plains of Shechem, addressing the Israelite congregation, he said, "Choose for yourselves this day whom you will serve. . . . But as for me and my house, we will serve the LORD" (Joshua 24:15 NKJV). A powerful proclamation, one that goes down in history as one of the best of all time. This section of the book will be intensely practical for men, dads, grandfathers, and fathers-to-be. For any moms reading this, I give you permission to turn off your husband's sports show and pass this book along to him to read. To quote from the movie *My Big Fat Greek Wedding*, "The man is the head, but the woman is the neck, and she can turn the head any way she wants." (Not biblical, but absolutely funny.)

In this proclamation from Joshua, the first thing I want you to take note of is that it is a *declaration*. He is declaring for himself and his household that they *will* serve the Lord. He's making a bold, strong declaration. Joshua is a strong man. He's a strong leader. He's a wonderful picture of what a father, a husband, a granddad ought to be. We need men like this today who will declare directly and powerfully, "We will, as a family, serve the Lord!" Now, Joshua might not have always been a strong leader. You might remember back in chapter 1 of Joshua, after Moses had died, that it was Joshua whom the Lord appointed to take control, to move up and step into Moses' shoes. Three times God would say to Joshua, "Be strong and very courageous." I don't know about you, but to me it seems that Joshua evidently needed this exhortation from the Lord and the responding encouragement from the congregation. Joshua's people wanted him to be strong. "So they answered Joshua, saying, 'All that you command us we will do, and wherever you send us we will go. . . . Only the LORD your God be with you as He was with Moses. . . . Only be strong and of good courage'" (1:16–18 NKJV). The people of Israel knew that strong leadership was the key. The same is true for America and the rest of the world. Strong leading fathers are the backbone of a society. Strong fathers create strong families, and strong families create a stronger country.

We need fathers today who will say, "This is what we're going to do." We live in a time when men are not taking a stand. Back in the day, moms would say, "Wait till your father comes home," and the kids would start to quake in their shoes. Nowadays, if kids heard that phrase, they'd probably scoff or shrug their shoulders because they know Dad never puts his foot down. The biblical example is men who say with strength and certainty, "We're not going to back away. This is the way it's got to be. As for me and my house, we will serve the Lord!" I'm not talking about chauvinism or brutality or being arrogant in personality, but about men who know how it's supposed to be and will say it with firmness.

Honking Horns and Flashing Lights

There was a story that came out on the news a few years back about a man named Michael Bryson. Michael and his wife, just a few months previously, had their first baby. Michael hadn't gotten used to taking care of a child, and like all parents with a newborn baby, he was sleep deprived (we can all relate to that). One morning, he put his baby in the car seat and temporarily put the car seat on top of the car while he cleaned out the car to make room for the new car seat. Once he was done cleaning, he got back in his car and drove off. A few minutes into his drive, he started noticing that everyone around him was honking their horns and flashing their lights at him. He didn't realize why everyone was freaking out around him until he made a stop and heard a loud clunk. Right then he realized what had just fallen off of the top of his car—his baby in the car seat. In a moment of terror, he bolted out of his car and ran frantically to the car seat on the side of the road. Miraculously, the car seat landed upright, and his baby was unharmed. The baby carrier did its job and so did God. Michael crumpled to the ground, overwhelmed with emotion, so thankful his son survived the forty-five-mile-an-hour ride. It was a miracle that his son was protected and even more of a miracle that Michael's wife didn't kill him for what he did.

As we're going down the highway of parenting in a daze, we too can do nutty things like Michael. We need honking horns and flashing lights to get our attention on what is severely wrong. A similar thing happened to Moses in Exodus 4. God had required that all the males of His children (the Jewish people) be circumcised as a sign of consecration and removal of the flesh. Moses had neglected to do that for his son, and we see in verse 24 that the Lord met him and sought to kill him. Yikes! Not often do we read about God seeking to kill one of

His servants, which means that this passage is a honking-horn and flashing-lights warning not only to Moses but to us.

Commentators say there might have been a couple of reasons why Moses neglected to circumcise his son: He was too busy, or his wife, who was a Midianite, did not follow the customs of the Jewish people and Moses was trying to simply appease her. Either way, Moses' big mistake was that he neglected to take the spiritual leadership of his home. God sought to kill Moses until his wife did the deed for him and God relented. God did not want Moses to lead three million Jewish people out of captivity until he focused on his most important ministry first—his own family.

It doesn't matter how many people you're impacting; the most important thing is your family. Moses almost died because he neglected his first ministry. His wife had to do what he was supposed to, and the situation was needlessly full of bitterness. Fathers, don't look for outside ministry if things aren't right with your family. This is your warning to step up to the plate and lead. Don't neglect your family. Don't compromise. Obey God's commands fully, no matter what the cost.

#Likeforlike

A lot of parenting today is rooted in sinful selfishness. Parents want their kids to like them and think they are cool. That is not what parenting is about. Oh, it's wonderful if and when our kids like us, but that's not the key. The key is to say, "It's not about you liking me or thinking I am cool; it's about raising you in the way that's going to be beneficial in the days to come and on into eternity."

In this social media day and age, you've probably heard of the popular hashtag "likeforlike." If you put that hashtag on a post, it indicates that if someone likes your post, then in return, you will like their post. In other words, if I like you, then you have to like me back. Unfortunately, this social media game does not work for parenting. A case in point is the biblical story of Eli and his sons.

Bible story time: Eli's downfall

In 1 Samuel we read about a priest named Eli and his sons, who were known in the community to be scoundrels without regard for the Lord. When the people would come in to make sacrifices, these men would treat the Lord's offering with contempt. Eli would hear of his sons' behavior but would do nothing about it. He casually talked to them on only one occasion, merely telling them that what they were doing was not right. He didn't put an end to it. He didn't remove them from the temple or discipline them. His sons knew their father was weak, and so they did not listen to him.

Shortly after, a man of God came to Eli and delivered a prophecy from the Lord against the house of Eli. He said that because he honored his sons more than God, his days would be shortened and both his sons would die (1 Samuel 2:27–34). Talk about a hardcore slap on the wrist. Eli might have been a little ahead of his time with the whole "likeforlike" social media phenomenon. In other words, Eli's downfall in parenting his sons was that he wanted his kids to like him more than he cared about what God thought of the whole situation. I have seen so many parents fall in this same way. They succumb to the fear of their kids not liking them. They will do whatever their kids want. They will buy whatever their kids ask for. They won't bring down the hammer when their kids are in the wrong. They want to be besties and "likeforlike" each other.

In an article for Focus on the Family, Sandra Stanley says there are four stages to parenting:

AS FOR ME AND MY HOUSE

1. Discipline: ages 0–5
2. Training: ages 5–12
3. Coaching: ages 12–18
4. Lifetime Friendship: ages 18 and up[6]

This list shows what should be the focus and foundation for each stage of your child's life. Notice that lifetime friendship is the very last stage. Now, don't get me wrong, there's nothing wrong with being best friends with your children in the prior stages of their life, but when that comes *before* honoring God it will be the downfall of you and your kids. A lot of mistakes are made when you bring friendship in too early with no discipline, training or coaching. This is perfectly depicted in the story of Eli and his children.

The primary goal for parents is to teach their children to *know* what's right and to *do* what's right in God's sight. If that means not compromising, giving lectures, grounding, and other discipline, then so be it. And if they dislike you in the process, so be it. We, as parents, must honor God more than we honor our kids. We think we're doing our kids good by letting them do whatever they want to keep them happy with us, but we are actually doing them great harm in the long run.

In Ephesians 6:1–4, Paul continues a call for harmony in the home to the Ephesian church. Here he addresses the children, knowing they would be in attendance. Why? Because Paul didn't view church as just a mom and dad thing, but for the children too. This is the key for good family life—be at church *together*.

Here is another key that kept our family together: Church was a way of life for us. Frank and I made it our mission that our family would not be in church just one day a week. This demonstrated to our kids that we put God first and valued being part of the body of Christ in a big way. We made sure that our family not only gathered together with God every day at home, but with the body of Christ during the week and on weekends. This went on even after our kids graduated from high school. My son and daughter went to a college that was not that far from us, and they came home to go to church, not only to attend but to serve. There were times they couldn't make it home, but they still made it a point to go to church somewhere nearby. Why? Because they had decided in their hearts that church was not just an event, but a way of life. That was how they were brought up, and they loved it.

A Tale of Two Families

There is an amazing, true story about two men: one who followed after God, walked in the fear of the Lord and obedience, and took his family to church; and another who didn't do it God's way. The documented history of the generations that followed them is a lesson impossible to miss.

It started in 1874, when Richard Dugdale, on behalf of the New York Prison Commission, began to visit state prison facilities and discovered a particular family connection between some of the inmates in Ulster County. (Interestingly, a descendant of Jonathan Edwards was president of this commission, but we will get to the Edwards's connection later.) Dugdale traced the lineage of these inmates to a man of Dutch ancestry named Max, born in 1720 in the Hudson Valley. In 1877, Dugdale published his findings in a study entitled *The Jukes: A Study in Crime, Pauperism, Disease, and Heredity*.[7] Juke was the name he gave to the family whose real name he did not wish to disclose. Dugdale estimated that there were 1,200 members of this family tree, and he was able to report on the details of 540 of these descendants, plus another 169 who married into the family line. One member of the family tree was said to be

Ada Juke, who married one of Max's sons, and was nicknamed "Margaret, Mother of Criminals." Of the total group of related individuals, Dugdale found that

- 310 were paupers who spent a combined 2,300 years in poorhouses,
- 130 were convicted criminals,
- 50 women were prostitutes, and
- 7 were murderers.

These paupers and criminals cost the state of New York $1.5 million to pay for their incarcerations and $1.25 million in public welfare and other costs to society apart from incarceration.

In 1900, Albert Edward Winship published a supplemental study, titled *Jukes-Edwards: A Study in Education and Heredity*. This one traced the descendants of America's leading theologian, Jonathan Edwards, and compared them with the Jukes family. The results were fascinating. He reported that out of approximately 1,400 known descendants of the Edwards family tree, there were

- virtually no lawbreakers;
- more than 100 lawyers and 30 judges;
- 13 college presidents, 100-plus professors;
- 100 clergymen, missionaries, and theological professors;
- 62 physicians;
- 80 elected public officials, including 3 mayors, 3 governors, several congressmen, 3 senators, and 1 vice-president;
- 60 authors or editors with 135 books to their credit; and
- 75 army or navy officers.[8]

What a difference between these two family lines! Edwards followed after God, walked in the fear of the Lord, and made it a priority that his family would follow after the things of God (read His Word, go to church, serve others, tithe). On the other hand, Juke led a life apart from the things of God, and the domino effect in his lineage produced nothing good. This goes to show that the actions a father takes in his home and in his own walk with the Lord will affect not only his family, but generations to come. In fact, their actions not only affected the family line, but the society around them. This is why fathers must take a stand to declare over themselves, their families, and the generations to come, "As for me and my house, we *will* serve the Lord."

Insights from Frank

In Joshua chapter 7, we read about a man named Achan. He was part of Israel's army under Joshua, and after a victorious battle, Achan stole the goods from the spoils of war and hid them under his tent. Because of his sin, not only was Achan stoned, but so were his kids and his wife. His family didn't steal like he did, but they experienced the deadly repercussions. What Achan did in secret affected his whole family. What happens in the minds of my kids, my grandkids, and my family when they overhear a conversation I have on the phone or with my wife? What are they really hearing? What are they really seeing? They're following in my footsteps, for better or for worse.

Twenty-plus years ago, I heard a story from a man who was sharing his testimony, how he loved the Lord but had also liked to drink. It wasn't that he was an alcoholic, but he enjoyed his alcohol. He lived in Chicago, and on Thanksgiving Day, when the snow was falling, after the family feast was done, he wanted some wine. After finding none in his liquor cabinet, he put on his hat, coat, and boots, and he went outside to walk to a liquor store three blocks away. He was halfway there when he sensed that somebody was following him. He turned around, and there was his four-year-old son with his hat and coat, taking great big giant steps, putting his feet in the newly fallen snow where his father had left footprints.

"Hey, buddy, what are you doing?" he said to his little boy.

The four-year-old said, "Daddy, I'm just walking in your footsteps."

The man realized that his son was walking in his footsteps as he went to the liquor store, and he asked himself, "Is that what I want for my boy?" At that moment he decided that he would never drink again. Together, he and his son walked back home.

Here's the deal: It's not that he was being legalistic. Because sure, he could have continued to drink. But his decision came with the question, Do I want my kids to do the same? Our kids may not have the same willpower as we do, or that we think we do. So ask yourself, *Do I want my kids to go there?* No? Then don't do it. You might say, "They don't see me. It doesn't matter." What happens in secret comes out openly. Who we are and what we do will affect our families. Our children are going to become like us.

This also applies to disciplining. If you want your kids to receive correction rightly, it starts with your walk. If you're growling, they'll resent it. But if you're spending time with the Father, your perspective changes. You are modified. Kids will know intuitively. They will know that we have been with Jesus and our disciplining of them comes from being in the Spirit and not in the flesh. They'll receive the Spirit, but the flesh they'll resent.

The Word of God says, "Do not be deceived, God is not mocked; for whatever a man sows, that he will also reap" (Galatians 6:7 NKJV). If you haven't had children yet, know that your future kids are going to be just like you. In other words, if you're being obnoxious, if you're being rude, if you're being rebellious, if you're being unspiritual, ungodly, deceptive, untruthful, whatever it might be, it's going to come back to you. I promise you. What you sow will always come back your way. Do you want your kids to be like you? If you say, "Not really," then change today! Repent. Even teens need to realize that they'd better count the cost: If they're tricking Mom or being sneaky, it's going to come back their way. Don't be deceived. Whatever you sow, whatever you plant, you will reap. Guaranteed.

As the spiritual leader of the home, Dad, you have to have a realization: It starts with me. What I do in secret is going to affect my family and my relationship with the Lord. There are things that need to be changed in me. Let this be your prayer: "Lord, today, alert me to the negative things in my life that are going to impact my sons or my daughters or my grandkids. Give me strength to turn away from them."

The time is now, men and women. The time is now to become strong like Joshua. God will bless you and your family as you do. The apostle John said, "I have no greater joy than to hear that my children are walking in the truth" (3 John 1:4). Nothing else matters in comparison to looking at your kids and grandkids and saying to yourself, *They're walking in truth. They love the Lord. They're on fire. They're being used by God.* No success in ministry or career can begin to hold a candle to that.

As a young Christian man, I was challenged by a song by Bob Dylan. In that very distinctive Dylan style, he sang about choosing whom you will serve. In the same way, our Lord challenged me through Joshua's declaration, "Choose this day whom you will serve!" I chose Jesus, and I have no regrets. Especially when I see the results in my son and daughter: They truly love the Lord with all their hearts; are walking in wisdom, in faith, and in the Spirit; and are loving God and people. I have no greater joy!

This is serious business, and it takes a serious decision to choose here and now—there is no middle ground—you will serve somebody. It may be the devil or it may be the Lord, but you will serve somebody. I pray you choose the latter.

Home Field Advantage

My family and I love football. Our favorite NFL teams are the Green Bay Packers and the Seattle Seahawks. Every sports fan knows that whenever your team is playing at home, they will have the advantage to win—that is what we call a home field advantage. The same can be applied to parenting. The home gives the advantage to the parent to train and disciple their children in the way they should go. Parents, make it a priority to have dinner as often as you can with your family and talk to them about Jesus. Make sure to have family devotionals together at least once a week. Teach them how to walk in the fear of the Lord and in wisdom and prudence. When you train them well at home, they'll go out and succeed in the "away games."

The way that the public-school systems are going these days, parents should really be praying about whether their kids should be homeschooled or attend private school. If you find out that their public school is teaching them the exact opposite of what you're teaching them at home (homosexuality, safe sex outside marriage, endless numbers of genders, creator-less evolution), then it's time to make a bold change. Making a sacrifice for your kids will be well worth it in the end.

Beat the Enemy to the Punch

Take advantage of the home field and beat the enemy to the punch by talking to your kids about *everything*—dads to sons and moms to daughters. The enemy would love nothing more than to get to your kids at an early age, because then he'll have years to build on that mindset, addiction, and sin. Tackle it head-on. Let their formative foundation be about truth rather than lies. All of this happens in the home. To combat the enemy, we need to create an environment with our kids where they can come to us about anything they've encountered or are struggling with. You can't control or shield everything from your kids; that's why parents should already be talking to their kids about their anatomy and sexuality as early as age five. Give your kids the truth so that they will already know what's right and what's wrong when they are exposed to any sexual content or issues of identity. Address it with the Word of God, which is Truth. The Truth will always trump lies. We live in a very sexualized world where the enemy is blatantly running around; we, as parents, need to make sure that we are beating the enemy to the punch by giving our kids the truth of the Word of God. First Peter 5:8 says, "Be alert and of sober mind. Your enemy the devil prowls around like a roaring lion looking for someone to devour." Be mindful of what's going on around you. There's an identity crisis that the enemy is trying to throw at our children. It's our job as parents to address it and give our kids the weapons and tools to combat the lies.

Being silent when it comes to the topic of sex is setting your kids up for destruction. Without the Truth implanted early in their lives, they will get a distorted view from the world and the enemy. This is why you need to have ongoing conversations with your kids about sex and their sexuality.

Explain to them that a sexual relationship is best when it is an intimate, private relationship between a husband and wife. Anything else results in problems and an eating away of the soul. Explain to them that humans aren't animals but that we have a body, soul, and spirit. God designed sex to combine two souls into one, and if it's outside a marriage covenant, then it will rip apart the soul like ripping apart two pieces of paper superglued together. God is always ready to forgive and restore our souls, but there will always be repercussions for our sins.

If you handle this confidently and at the right time, you and your spouse will set up yourselves to be the ones your kids come to for answers about sexual issues. This will ultimately help empower them to live victoriously and purely in an over-sexualized culture.

Home-Front Talk: Anatomy

Talking about anatomy with your kids at an early age will help them feel comfortable with asking questions about it. When kids have a healthy attitude about their anatomy, they will grow a healthy attitude toward their sexuality. If you don't have the right words, there are great resources to turn to. For example, *The Story of Me* by Stan and Brenna Jones[9] is a great, God-centered book for kids that addresses anatomy, differences between male and female bodies, sex, and other things. All you have to do is read it through with them—ideally, father with son, mother with daughter. Seek out the many biblical resources available that will help you initiate open conversations with your kids. Remember to make it comfortable and natural. If you make it stiff, scary, or shameful, your kids will not seek you out to engage in conversation. You want them to talk to you openly and freely about their sexuality. You don't want them to be ashamed of anything about their bodies. You want them to have a wonder and reverence for them. And always remember to let them know that their bodies are ultimately temples of the Holy Spirit (see 1 Corinthians 6:19).

Home-Front Talk: What the Enemy Would Like Hidden

Don't make sex talks hidden or private all the time. Talk about hard topics like masturbation and pornography. Show them how not to awaken love before it's time (mentioned often in the Song of Solomon). Tell them plainly that sexual addiction can lead to a life of bondage and destruction. Let your kids know that they should not set any evil thing before their eyes and how things like pornography are wicked. It will leave them with a distorted view of how God intended sex to be within the context of marriage. We talked about sex with our kids when they were starting middle school, but now kids are getting exposed to it even as early as elementary school. Kids should now know everything about their anatomy and sexuality midway through elementary school. Start to talk to them then about sex and the other hard topics. This is how you beat the enemy to the punch. This is your home-court advantage.

Home-Front Talk: Competition and Sibling Rivalry

If you see comparison and sibling rivalry start to pop up in your home, tackle it head on by addressing the *heart* attitudes. Show your kids that the root of comparison is insecurity and fear. Tell them that everyone is going to have different talents, and some more than others, but that doesn't take away from you. Explain to them that they are all on the same team—the Jesus team. It's all for Him and for His glory. Make your kids experts in one another's strengths. Go around the dinner table and ask each child to say something that they love about another sibling. Parents, it's so important that you do not show favoritism for one child over another, nor compare them to each other. That will make your children compete for your love and affection. Let the Word of God renew their minds and bring to light their heart attitudes of fear, insecurity, jealousy, and pride. Give them Scripture that will renew their minds and transform their hearts. There's power in speaking the Word of God. Don't ever forget that.

Play the Long Game

In parenting, you have to not only be thinking about your home discipleship, but how outside influences of school and friendships can affect your kids in the long run. In sports, playing the long game means thinking ahead, and in this case, we need to be strategizing and creating environments for our kids that will help them stay in the community of faith. Here are some key things we did to foster that environment.

First, have your church pour into your kids. Having young adult mentors is so key, especially in their preteen and teenage years. Having someone of the same sex, who is a few years older, take your child under his or her wing to mentor them on a regular basis is huge. Parents telling their child a certain truth is sometimes not nearly as powerful as when someone else tells them—especially if it comes from someone they look up to. Your children's friends matter so much because who they hang around is who they'll become. You can't control who their friends are, but you can create an atmosphere of church circles and mentors so they are hanging around the right kind of influence. Put your kids in an environment where the Holy Spirit is most likely to work. That is Spirit-filled parenting.

Second, establish an environment of asking for forgiveness. I'm not exaggerating when I say that my husband and I apologized more to our kids than they did to us. We owned up to our mistakes. This modeled for them authenticity, humility, and how to apologize and repent. Apologizing obliterates any hypocrisy in your life. Let's face it, we all know that hypocrisy is the fastest way for your kids to rebel and turn away from Jesus and the church. Your kids know that you're not perfect, so when you own up to your mistakes, it will make them see that your faith is legit and Jesus is real. Asking for forgiveness will ultimately prepare your kids to accept Jesus in their hearts by surrender, repentance, and acceptance. Your simple "I'm sorry" can usher your kids into the Kingdom of God. This is how you can play the long game in parenting. And ultimately, this is how you foster a house of spiritual leadership and home-front discipleship.

As the famous saying goes, "If you want to change the world, go home and love your family."[10]

The Key

If you're a parent who feels overwhelmed about the things that your children are or will be facing in such a perverted and confusing culture, remember this: *God created and fashioned them for such a time as this.* Know that God has given our children a spirit inside of them that is beyond powerful. Just continue to get them in the atmosphere where they can encounter God—whether that be mission trips, outreaches, house churches, small groups, or with godly mentors. That's the difference maker. And be very aware of what secular public education is teaching your children. Either keep them away from public school, or if they must go, then make sure they are thoroughly equipped with what is true and what is false. Teach them the Word and what God says about gender, sex, and even the truth about our nation's history and how it was founded upon the Bible and God. Overall, this is key: Don't parent from fear, know that God's got you and your kids, but also use wisdom.

PUT IT INTO PRACTICE:
SPIRITUAL LEADERSHIP AND HARD TOPICS

- Make a family mission statement (like a coat of arms) and put it up in your house as a daily reminder. Example: Garcia Family Mission Statement—We bring faith, hope, and love to those who are in need. We are humble, kind, and fearless. We serve people, love greatly, give generously, and share the Gospel wherever we go.
- Put up a chalkboard or whiteboard in your house and write down all the ways the Lord has been faithful, including miracles in your family's lives. (In Exodus, after God provided manna in the wilderness, God told

Moses to put some in an omer so that it might be kept for generations, so they would remember God's power and faithfulness to them.) Write down your testimonies as parents and allow the kids to write down ways that the Lord answered their prayers or revealed Himself to them.

- Talk to your kids early about anatomy, sexuality, pornography, and masturbation. Create a safe environment where they can come to you about anything. Ask the Holy Spirit to give you insight into what may be secretly going on in their lives.

- Keep your children in a community of faith, surrounded by the right mentors and friendships.

- Spend one hour a week with all devices off and teach your children something about American history and the Bible. There are some amazing resources out there to help, like those at hillsdale.edu.

9

DON'T MOLD, UNFOLD

Unfolding Who God Created Your Child to Be

One of my favorite scenes from the movie *Shrek* is the scene where Shrek is explaining that there's more to ogres than big scary monsters.

He says, "Ogres are like onions," to which Donkey wisecracks, "They stink? They make you cry? Or you leave them out in the sun and they get all brown and start sprouting little white hairs?"

Shrek, irritated, says, "No! Layers! Onions have layers. Ogres have layers. We both have layers."

Just like ogres and onions, humans also have layers. God created each child with unique giftings, abilities, and passions, and it's up to the parent to take time to unfold those layers, one piece at a time. We were not meant to mold them into what we want them to be, but to unfold what God created them to be.

Did you notice that Proverbs 22:6 says we are to train up our children in the way they should go, not in the way we wish they would go? My husband will admit that men are particularly vulnerable to making their sons walk in the way they wish they would go. Just because you, Dad, played football in high school doesn't mean your son should. Or just because you have a family business that you started from the ground up, doesn't mean your son has to follow in your footsteps and take it over. We see this happen all the time, fathers pressuring their sons to take up a trade that they themselves are good at, but it isn't their son's passion. Or fathers wanting their sons to play a certain sport that they played so they can selfishly relive the glory days through their sons. (Think Uncle Rico from *Napolean Dynamite*, who was stuck so much in the glory days that he truly believed he could "throw a pigskin over them mountains.") Ever notice that it's always the dads who sit around and talk about how they used to play and what they used to do? Nobody else cares. I mean, in fact, the other dads don't even care. They're just waiting to tell their story. Sadly, all too often children are pressured in a certain direction. What parents are doing is mold-ing their children into something that the child might not have been created to do. Wise are the father and mother who study their kids carefully to see how the Lord made them specifically, because parenting is not so much about molding as it is about unfolding.

A perfect biblical example of this is when Saul dresses David for battle in 1 Samuel 17. David had just declared that he would fight Goliath, so Saul brings David into his tent and puts his armor on him, thinking that if it works for him, it will work for David. Saul was trying to mold David into the warrior he wanted him to be—dressed in garments and armor that he wore. But you see, God doesn't always work like that. He gives each of us unique talents, giftings, abilities, and passions that, put together, are different from any other person's. David wouldn't have been able to conquer Goliath the way God wanted him to if he had gone out to battle in someone else's armor. The passage here says that he wasn't even able to walk in it, let alone slay a giant (verse 39). Once David removed Saul's mold, and took his shepherd's staff and stones, he was freer and much more able to defeat Goliath through the power of God.

Colossians 3:21 (AMPC) says, "Fathers, do not provoke or irritate or fret your children [do not be hard on them or harass them], lest they become discouraged and sullen and morose and feel inferior and frustrated. [Do not break their spirit.]" This Scripture shows us that we can provoke and discourage our children by torturing them with expectations. Parents have a tendency to say, "Here's what you're going to do"—don't do that. Don't provoke your children to anger and cause them to say, "Man, my dad just expects so much of me, and I'm not him." Parents forcing their kids to live their unfulfilled dreams only cause consternation in the child. We are discovering that children are not to be molded. They're to be unfolded. Parents, you have the privilege of observing your kids carefully and seeing how God made them, and then unfolding what God has built into them from the moment of birth. If you try to make your kids do something they were not designed to do, they will become discouraged, depressed, and angry. And in later years, you're going to feel the anger of your child. "How come Mom made me?" Or "Why did Dad force me?" Or "Why couldn't my parents just let me be?"

Wise are the parents who do not provoke their kids to anger or discouragement. What Colossians 3:21 is essentially saying is, "Lord, how did You make this child? How did You design him or her? Help me to get behind what You've built into them."

Insights from Sarah

If someone asked me if I believe in miracles, I would say yes—I *am* a miracle. As mentioned in my mom's testimony, my mom was told by doctors that she couldn't have kids. So the fact that we were born is a miracle in itself. She had the faith that God would bless her with children, and she knew in her heart her children would be used by God. Just like Hannah in the Bible, who couldn't have kids—she prayed a bold prayer and told God that if He blessed her with a child, she would offer him or her up to Him in service. My mom knew my brother and I had a special calling on our lives, so she did everything in her power to nurture us, disciple us, and make sure she was unfolding everything that God had designed in us. She paid special attention to what we naturally gravitated toward and what our passions and interests were.

My brother loved to play with Legos and computers. My mom saw that and fostered an environment that encouraged his interests. My mom saw I was creative and adventurous, so she gave me opportunities to grow in that. She also saw that we both loved music, so she put us in music classes. Those things that she observed to be innately in us were the very things that we grew up to be. My brother is an electrical/computer engineer, inventor, and musician. And I'm a business owner and entrepreneur, and I love the Word of God so much, I have a master's degree in it. Oh yeah, and we both lead worship. My dad played football growing up, but he never once forced my brother to play just because he played. He saw that his son preferred staying indoors and inventing things. My mom didn't force me to be a teacher like she was, but saw that I had a gift for coming up with new ideas and implementing them. Instead of molding us, they unfolded everything that God had designed us to do. Because of this, we were free and happy to do what our passions were. Parents often push their children into professions that make good money, because they want them to have a solid career. But if the son or daughter does not have a passion for that profession, and does it just to please his or her parents, they will end up unhappy and restless because they are not doing what they were designed by God to do. If you don't know what your kids are supposed to do, then let them try a bunch of things and see what makes them excited. Prayer is also a big component in this. Pray each day that the Holy Spirit will open your eyes to the way God designed them to be. That He will show you what you should foster and focus on in your children.

Insights from Sal

You know by now that I really liked playing with Legos growing up. What really captured my imagination was the ability to go "off script," to make whatever my mind dreamed of making without having to stay within the confines of the instruction manual. The picture on the box might have shown a NASA space shuttle, but I already knew in my mind that it was going to be a submarine that could travel into volcanoes and journey to the core of the earth to save the princess from the evil lava monster (hey, I should try to get a movie deal for that story!). The point is, I viewed every Lego set as a pile of building blocks with which I could build whatever I could dream up. I didn't feel forced to follow the set of instructions, or ever feel like I had to tell myself, "No, it has to be built only in this way." The same is true for raising children. Parents lovingly provide the building blocks, then the child builds his or her life with those blocks, in a natural way, without being forced into what the parents think that life should look like. In that way, the child has the freedom to dream up a life, a career, a faith, and a future, all on their own. The parents just have to make sure to provide the best building blocks—character, faith, honesty, compassion, and a good work ethic.

Identity—Knowing *Whose* You Are

Social media has taken over the world. If we're bombarded by so many social media platforms now, how much more prevalent will it be in the next few years? It's crazy to think about. Statistics show that internet users spent an average of two hours and forty-five minutes per day on social networking. That's an enormous amount of time letting the customs and cultures of this world shape your identity and worldview. Social media has a way of affecting our identity, which is why the topic of identity needs to be addressed. Teaching your kids their identity will be the catalyst for a grounded future for them—everything in life is predicated upon identity. There is a real trend going on right now that pushes young kids to self-identify. It says that you need to know who you are, right now, in the most awkward stage of your life. When I was in junior high, if someone asked me to self-identify I probably would have said I was a dolphin. I don't know why we are doing this to people, but there is a better identity than any we could put on ourselves, and it's God-given. How do we teach our kids about their God-given identity? To find out, let's take a look at a story in the Bible that exemplifies this so well.

In Matthew 16, Jesus decides to give His disciples a little pop quiz and asks them who people say that He is. Simon says that He's the Christ, the Son of the Living God. Then Jesus changes Simon's name to Peter and says that on this Rock He will build His Church. Here is the revelation in this story: The more we know God, the more He reveals to us. Peter's name was once Simon, which means sifting sand. Simon was all over the place before he met Jesus, always saying the wrong things and putting his foot in his mouth. After he spent time with Jesus and began to really know Him, the more he saw who he was in Christ. After Simon responded to Jesus that He is the Christ, the Son of God, Jesus then gave Simon a new name: Peter, which means rock. He went from shifting sand to a solid, firm rock. In effect, Jesus was telling Peter, "After the Father revealed who I really am, I'm going to tell you who you really are."

It's important to teach your children who they are in Christ— not only will this draw them closer to God in an intimate way, but they will know not to listen to Satan and his lies. There is much danger these days in children, teens, and even young adults not knowing the truth of God's love and purpose for them—so there's much confusion, depression, and even suicide. God's plans for them are much bigger and better than they can think or even imagine! In fact, God's plan for them began long before they were born.

When we talk to our kids about identity and who they are in Christ, it's important to share with them that they were created in God's image. Yet, because of Adam and Eve's rebellion, we now all have a sin nature. But God, in His great love and grace, offered us salvation through the last perfect and final sacrifice of His Son, Jesus, on the cross. Share the plan of salvation again if you need to. Those who were far from God become His very dwelling place. Those who once were objects of God's wrath have become the beloved bride of Christ (see Ephesians 2:1–5).

That is their glorious new identity. Show them that they are not who they used to be—no matter what they feel or who others say they are. They are who God says they are!

This should be their sole identity. Let your children know their position in Christ and who God says they are.

- Chosen: You were handpicked by God. (Ephesians 1:4)
- Forgiven: All your sins were forgiven before God. God will not condemn you. (Ephesians 1:6–8)
- Redeemed: Your life debt is covered, and you can look forward to the rich purpose God has for you. (Ephesians 1:13–14)
- Loved: You are deeply loved. In fact, God gave you His most precious gift—His Son, Jesus. (Romans 8:39)
- Accepted: You have been welcomed by God into His family. (Romans 15:7)

After learning all these amazing, foundational truths, there are many descriptive names for those who have put their faith in Christ. The following are just a few.

- Children of God: John 1:12, Romans 8:14–16. Through the finished work of Christ, God—by His grace and through our faith—adopts us into His family.
- Members of His household: Ephesians 2:19.
- Part of the family of believers: Galatians 6:10. In Christ, God becomes knowable to us as a perfect heavenly Father (see Matthew 7:9).
- Beloved: Romans 9:25. Jesus tells us that the Father loves us just as the Father loves Jesus Himself (see John 17:23).
- One with God, through Christ: John 17:23.

- The Elect: Matthew 24:22, 2 Timothy 2:10. In His mysterious plan, God graciously chose us to experience salvation and all its amazing benefits.
- Disciples: Matthew 28:19. We are students of Christ, following Him in order to know Him and His teaching, grow to be like Him, and go with Him on the mission to make other disciples.
- Children of promise: Galatians 4:28. Our new birth is a miracle, like Abraham's son Isaac's. It is God's doing, not something we make happen like Ishmael's birth (see Genesis 16). Christians are "children of the free woman" (Galatians 4:31).
- Conquerors: Romans 8:37. Paul writes, "We are more than conquerors," because of Christ. Because of our union with Jesus, we share in His complete victory over sin, death, and the devil.
- Citizens of heaven: Philippians 3:20. Since our true home is far away in heaven, a believer's ultimate allegiance is to God and His Kingdom—not the world around us.
- The Church: Matthew 16:18. With all the others who have trusted Christ, we compose a new, living organism of which Christ is the head.

Show your kids that what Jesus says about them should be their sole identity and where their security is found. So many kids develop a performance mentality because they don't know their true identity in Christ, and the only support and praise they receive comes when they perform well. This develops a belief that in order to receive love or any sort of attention, they need to perform well. The result of this flawed belief will be much fear and anxiety in kids, because they are living their life for the approval of people rather than God. Teach your kids that people's approval of them will always change, but God's love for them will never change regardless of how well they perform. Let that belief and message be ingrained in your children. This will give them so much security, and it will be the foundation of their identity as they grow up.

Who You Are When No One Is Looking

The great John Wooden once said, "Be more concerned with your character than your reputation, because your character is what you *really* are, while your reputation is merely what others *think* you are."[1] And, "The true test of a man's character is what he does when no one is watching."[2]

We, as parents, want our children to act in godly ways when no one is watching. In order for that to happen, they must have good character. Building godly character in your kids is one of the best things you can do to prepare them for life. It is so easy to get caught up making sure that our kids are well educated and good in academics and that they develop skills in sports or music, while ignoring the importance of character building. As parents, it is our responsibility to work diligently at helping our children develop and grow in character. If parents were to work on their children's character and make that their sole focus, everything else (grades, relationships, sports) would fall into place. Parents, don't put so much stress on things that don't really matter in the long run. All you have to do is help your children become who God intended them to become—someone rooted in God's Word who has strong biblical character. Parents are the best equipped for this job because they love their children more than anyone else does, and they also know their kids better than anyone else does.

If there is one thing lacking in our society today, it is godly character. This is why it is so vital that parents have a vision for raising a generation of young people with good, strong Christian character, who will stand out in the world and be used by God.

Romans 13:14 says, "Put on the Lord Jesus Christ" (NKJV). Christlikeness is an excellent definition of character. God didn't say this as a suggestion. It was a command, which means it must be very important to the Lord.

Throughout this book, we've seen some examples of how we can instill character in our children. In chapter 3, we saw how our children learn character by our example. If we exemplify godly character, then they will exemplify godly character. Children learn character every day through the models that they look up to. This is why it's important for us to make sure that the entertainment our kids are watching, the books they are reading, the friends they are hanging out with, and the people that they look up to exemplify godly character. We've also seen that our children learn character through discipline and through the teaching of the Word of God. All of these topics are intertwined in character building. Now we're going to dive deeper into some common ways we can continue to help our children build godly character.

Do Hard Things

Did you know that by not having your kids do hard things, you are weakening and crippling them? If you stop going to the gym, stop working out your muscles, and stop building strength, you're going to have a weak body that is susceptible to disease and injuries. The same goes for parenting. My generation (the baby boomer generation) decided that it was going to do the opposite of what our parents did. Our parents' generation went through the world wars and had it ingrained in them to be tough and well-disciplined. My generation (who became the hippy generation) decided to rebel against that and make things easy when it came to parenting. This meant giving our children everything they wanted and doing everything for them. My generation invented helicopter parenting, and "everybody wins" when it came to competitions. This "soft" parenting ended up backfiring on us, as we now see entitlement and lack of stamina to overcome hard things. The millennial generation and the generations after them have not been tested the way the generations before them have been—who were able to endure World War I and World War II. They never knew what it was like to storm the beaches of Normandy, knowing that they likely weren't coming back alive. Or to pick themselves up by their britches during the Great Depression and get things moving again. Granted, some millennials, and those that came after, have lived hard lives. But most have had everything handed to them, and all of the information of the world is accessible at the tips of their fingers. It has created weak children.

The remedy for this, in regard to parenting, is to have your children do hard things. You can counter the culture and counter the world's philosophy to just get by, by instilling in them grit, gumption, and great endurance. The three Gs.

A person who perfectly exemplifies this kind of character and upbringing is the amazing governor of South Dakota, Kristi Noem. If you haven't heard of her, look her up. She's inspiring (and has very sculpted arms, I might add). Kristi grew up with a dad who was tough. He was a cowboy. He woke her and her siblings up every day by yelling up the stairs, "Get up! More people die in bed than anywhere else!" They were always "burning daylight."[3] They had to be in a hurry everywhere they went, and they worked all the time. She would have to do hard work on the farm before going to school in the early morning and hard work after school. It was tough, but it made her into the woman that she is today. Kristi recounts in a speech that it was a remarkable way to grow up. It instilled in her grit, perseverance, and business smarts.

When we take these opportunities away from our kids, we are inevitably crippling them. What made America great were the legal immigrants who came to this country, who started from the ground up to make a living, start a business, and raise a family. They had nothing handed to them, and all odds were stacked against them, but they took advantage of the freedoms they had in this country and got to work.

Going through hard times is what makes you a problem solver. It is an opportunity to learn that you can do hard things—it gives you confidence. By doing everything for their children, parents are not allowing them to be people who can get through life's difficulties and be successful.

When you are raising children, allow them to be responsible for what's going on in their lives. Give them chores. If they need money to go shopping, have them work for it by mowing the neighbor's lawn. Let them make their own peanut butter and jelly sandwiches. Let them have the hard conversations with their teachers instead of interfering and doing it for them. Give them difficult challenges, because when they figure it out, they will become problem solvers, and they will have the confidence to take on anything that hits them in life. Remember what the Bible says in Romans 5:3–4: "We also glory in our sufferings, because we know that suffering produces perseverance; perseverance, character; and character, hope."

Insights from Sarah

While we were growing up, my dad was an example of how hard work and determination can propel you into your dreams. When my parents got married, they had little to no money. My dad didn't even have a high school diploma, but that didn't stop him from getting to work. He decided to learn the trade of concrete construction and got really good at it. He would wake up before the sun came up every morning and would work hard to build his business. He taught us not to make excuses for any situation we were in, but to get to work and do it as unto the Lord. My parents encouraged us to get good grades and excel in whatever we were doing. They taught us to work, and then enjoy the fruits of our labor afterward. When I had an idea to start a clothing company, even when people were discouraging me from starting it, my parents encouraged me to take a risk and go for it. It was hard work, but the character and the confidence that they instilled in me growing up helped me to not give up.

Smartphones: Not the "Smart" Way

The last way to build character in our kids is by ditching the smartphones during their formative and teenage years. Our society is very quickly losing the essential skill of confident communication, and smartphones are largely to blame for that. Smartphones are destroying our humanity by taking away our communication and confident relational interaction. We now have the least orally and verbally communicative generation in American history. Typing, texting, video games, and social media are all contributors to a voiceless generation. We have to break free from this slavery that comes with smartphones.

Parents, here's a basic rule of thumb: No child under the age of eighteen should have a smartphone. Simple as that. Smartphones were developed and designed largely to become the one thing you cannot live without. Did you know that Facebook, Google, and Apple have child neuroscientists that work for them? Their job is to figure out ways to attract and motivate your child to engage in longer periods of screentime.

Some have accused these companies of "deliberately creating addictive products."[4] For example, they intentionally create the swipe down feature with your finger to resemble that of a slot machine motion so that each time you swipe, it releases dopamine in your brain to see what you will get (likes, messages, feeds from friends). Not only do smartphones cause addiction, but they cause depression, because you're watching someone else's highlight reel while you're sitting in your pajamas on the couch doing nothing. They're manufactured to be addictive. They cause depression, and they make evil things like pornography and pedophilia easily accessible. Does this sound like something you want to give your kids, especially under the age of eighteen? I don't think so. Childhood and teenage years are the most formative years, and the best time to instill godly attributes, character, and habits. Really pray about whether you should give your children smartphones. There are alternate ways for your kids to stay in contact with their friends through phone calls and text messaging (like Jitterbug, for example). A suggested game plan is to allow them a phone in their preteen and teenage years, but one with which they can call and text only. Once they're eighteen, they can receive a smartphone. For social media, we would encourage kids to not have accounts, unless they need one for a job. But if you have already prayed about it and feel like your children can handle it, before they go away to college, mentor them and show them how to use it in a way that involves discipline, awareness, and wisdom. This is a quintessential way in which we can build character into our kids and set them up for success in the long run.

PUT IT INTO PRACTICE:
UNFOLDING AND INSTILLING

- Be creative and resist the urge to mold your children. Unfold who God created them to be by having them try various activities to unfold their passions, giftings, and skills.

- Teach your kids the dangers of a culture that pushes "self-identification," which has its roots in pride. Also teach them how social media can lead to being ensnared in comparison, insecurity, and addiction. Let God awaken them to who they really are through the truth of His Word.

- Let them know their position and their identity in Christ. Put a copy of the identity declarations earlier in this chapter in a visible place in your house. Consider declaring them together at breakfast or another mealtime.

- Write this declaration down for yourself and speak and prophesy it over your kids regularly: My kids will not grow up tormented, demonized, gender-confused, addicted, or unsure of who they are. They will be sons and daughters of God who know their identity and purpose, pursuers of God's heart, and restorers of those who are broken.

- Make a commitment to have your kids do hard things.

- Monitor and come up with a game plan for your children who are living in a technological world.

10

LEGOS AND KITCHENS

Parenting Roles through Structure and Nurture

Some little girls dream of becoming president of the United States. Do you want to know why I never did when I was young? Because I pictured what being the president might look like: Every morning, before you can even wake up nicely, someone taps you on the shoulder and whispers, "Problems—all kinds of problems." Such a nice way to start each morning.

Life is full of problems. The first recorded problem we see in the Bible is in Genesis 2, when God says, "It is not good for man to be alone" (verse 18). God knew mankind was missing part of the equation, so He created a woman. God, in His infinite wisdom, knew man would need a helpmate (woman) to complement his weaknesses and that the woman would need the same.

The male and female genders were profoundly designed by God to be different for a reason. Those differences would make the role of a father and a mother effective together in raising children. That is why the family (as God designed it) is so important when it comes to raising children. There has never been a more important time than now for us to operate in our God-given gender. Lisa Bevere, a renowned speaker and author, wisely said, "I believe houses are the healthiest when they have both the voice of a father and a voice of a mother. And together, those two can have one heart and speak to the same purpose."[1]

Differences in Male and Female Strengths

So what are the differences between male and female strengths, and how does God use both for parenting and raising up godly children? Let me preface this by saying that these categories are not always the case, but in *general* men and women can be geared toward these characteristics.

In my family, my husband and my son have a more structural and compartmental mindset. For example: I raised a son who loved to play with Legos. Whenever we went to the store, Sal pleaded with us to get him a Lego set. Every year, his Christmas wish was Legos. And he wouldn't just go for the small Legos, no sir. He went straight for the biggest Lego box his little six-year-old arms could wrap around—like the *Star Wars Death Star* or the *Millennium Falcon*. My husband and I would joke that we would have to take out a loan to buy all the Lego sets he wanted, because Legos weren't cheap. My son also loved to stack all of his Legos up high and make it look like one big Jenga tower. He then pushed them over, giggling when the Legos came crashing down into a million pieces and sprayed across the room. (My feet have yet to recover from accidentally stepping on those Legos.)

Like all twins, if one is having fun doing something, the other wants in on the action. One day, during their playtime, my son was off stacking his Legos, and my daughter decided to join in. Instead of playing with his Legos, she brought her miniature kitchen set with her and started to use her brother's *Star Wars* Lego action figures in her pretend kitchen. When her brother asked her where she put his *Star Wars* Lego action figures, she pointed to her miniature oven and said that they were in the oven baking. Her brother was mortified that she would take his precious Legos and bake them. Poor Anakin Skywalker, always getting burned. It's a funny story to look back on, but as I was thinking about it, my little six-year-old girl, by playing house, was simply exemplifying what many girls are good at, and that is *nurturing*. In many cases, men are geared toward structure, and women are geared toward nurture. While men generally operate by structure, leadership, and guidance, women generally operate by connection, relationships, and creating environments in which people can flourish. Man's nature is often geared toward being protective of his household; woman's nature is often in tune with how to be protective of her children's hearts. Each has strengths that complement the other, and both are needed.

When we go all the way back to the garden with Adam and Eve, we see that when men and women are left alone, without the other to cover their weaknesses, we get the Fall. Because Eve was left alone, she became easily deceived by the serpent. When Adam saw what Eve had done, he knowingly took the fruit in disobedience. That's why the Bible says Adam's sin was the greater sin. Men and women need each other—to fill in the gaps. When one spouse is lacking in a certain area, the other's strength can help them in their weakness, and vice versa. This is why God's ideal plan is to have both the father and the mother engage in parenting. Roles are reversed in some cases, but the point is that *both* strengths are being applied to the children. When one parent is neglecting their part in parenting, the child will suffer. Well, you might ask, what about those single moms or dads out there who don't have a choice? That's where God comes in to meet those needs. He'll give that single parent guidance through His Word and bring mentors and church family to help in the uncovered areas. God always gives grace and mercy to help in times of need. This chapter, however, is a wake-up call to parents that haven't been doing their part in raising their children. In many cases, men think that their wives are to be the sole ones raising the kids, but nothing could be further from the truth. There are things that men can bring to the table that women can't and vice versa. Men and women need each other, especially in parenting.

Insights from Sarah

There's something so powerful when a mom gives her full attention, love, and care in raising her kids. That's my mom. She worked hard to get an education and a job, but when we were born, she left it to raise my brother and me. My brother and I went to school, yet she still tutored us afterward. She played with us, invested in us, and made sure to saturate us with the Word of God and worship music every minute she could. I wouldn't be the woman I am today without the sacrifice, love, and care she gave to me growing up. I always advise parents to make the financial sacrifice during the critical seasons of raising a child so that one of the parents can be home. Even if that means sizing down, like buying a smaller house or selling an extra car. Do whatever you can to be present with your kids. It will benefit them in the long run, beyond anything you can imagine.

My parents didn't have a newer car and didn't go out to restaurants often or take expensive vacations regularly. We would often just take simple camping trips. Looking back, those are the most meaningful memories. Once we were old enough to go to school, my mom got a part-time job or helped at our church when we were at school. Because she was a teacher, she was able to substitute at our school sometimes, and we were able to go to lunch with her. Most of my friends back then would tell me how blessed I was to have my mom. Many times, my friends wanted to be around my mom because they just needed that attention they didn't receive from theirs.

One thing that breaks my heart in regard to the family is the pursuit of money and getting ahead in careers at the expense of raising godly children. I believe this has caused so many divisions in the family. Men and women have God-given strengths innate in them to parent their children. The downfall, however, is when one parent decides to selfishly pursue a career for more money and comfort, and therefore is absent from raising their children. Each year in the United States, approximately one out of every ten young women between the ages of fifteen and nineteen becomes pregnant, a ratio that has changed little since 1973. According to the CDC, 16.7 per 1,000 teenage females became pregnant in 2019.[2] And what was the underlying connection in many of these homes? You guessed it—single-parent homes or absent mothers or fathers. Research shows that girls whose families are not intact are more apt to have sexual experiences at an early age.[3] If you're a single mom—don't give up hope. Even though the odds are against you, God can help you make up the difference in your family.

In light of this study, moms need to be thinking carefully. In Old Testament listings of the kings in Israel, you'll see a strong king followed by a wicked king. But the interesting point to note is that it's always the mother mentioned with the success or failure of the kings. This goes to show that both parents—mother *and* father—are crucial in raising godly children. This type of thinking goes against the way our culture operates. They think that in order to be successful in life, you must have a thriving career and many Instagram followers. We should not conform to the pattern of this world, but be transformed by the renewing of our mind regarding that matter. The most successful and important thing you can do is invest in your children and raise them up in the Lord. The greatest opportunity of your life is at your disposal. Training, watching, and discipling your kids is a priority. Both the father's and mother's strengths (structure and nurture) are needed in raising godly kids. Two are indeed better than one.

El Shaddai

In Bible study methods, there's a principle called *first mention*. When the Bible mentions a name or an appearance for the first time, you must look at the context, because it gives weight to the meaning of that name or appearance. In Genesis 17:1 (NKJV), God says to Abraham, "I am Almighty God; walk before Me and be blameless." This is the first mention of a new name for God and one that appears over and over again in the Bible. In

Hebrew, Almighty God means *El Shaddai*. What God is saying to Abraham here in this verse is that before He can give Abraham an exhortation to be perfect, He will give him revelation of His nature. Let's look at what El Shaddai means.

- El—the name of God that speaks of the right arm of a strong being. A bulging bicep. It's the idea of masculine might and power.
- Shaddai—Shad is a women's breast that is giving nourishment to an infant.

The combination is incredible. God is our strong, mighty, masculine One. He sees us through with the right hand of His strength. But He also will lovingly nurture you like a mother would with her infant baby. God's nature is that of both mighty masculinity and tender femininity, all wrapped up in one name: El Shaddai.

God is our Father, and if we, His children, need both of His natures in becoming perfect, then how much more should parents, male and female, be operating in their roles? The family needs dads to step up and be strong masculine leaders, and moms should not neglect their roles in being tender—physically, emotionally, and spiritually offering nourishment to their families. Both roles operating in unity is how God intended it to be. This is how the family looks most like God.

PUT IT INTO PRACTICE:
FATHER STRENGTHS, MOTHER STRENGTHS

- Make a commitment that you and your spouse will both participate in your God-given roles and strengths. If you are unsure what that looks like in a specific situation, make that a consistent matter of prayer.

- For all the single parents out there, remember, our heavenly Father is faithful and true. He hears your prayers for your daughters and sons. Do your best to seek out godly mentors for your children. The best place to look is at your home church.

11

THE CHASTENED CHILD

Training Children in the Way They Should Go

Insights from Sarah

Growing up, my parents would give us chewable vitamin Cs every morning before heading off to school. Instead of taking it, I would hide the tablet under our living room couch and hope no one would know. Everything was okay until one Christmas, to my demise, my parents decided to rearrange the living room furniture to fit our new Christmas tree. When they moved the couch, there, in all its glory, was a mound of vitamin Cs that had partly melted and permanently stained our nineties lime green carpet. Because that lie went on for a few months, my parents knew they needed to deal with it with discipline. Since this was a pretty big lie that had continued, instead of a time-out, they told me that I was going to get spanked. Now I was scared. So scared that I kept trying to make excuses—I was actually doing them a favor since now they had to get rid of that hideous lime green carpet. But my parents didn't have it. Instead, my dad took me to my room and got out the infamous Ping-Pong paddle. I remember him being calm but stern and explaining to me why I was going to get spanked. He said that lying and being sneaky was sinful, and since this was a continuous sin, I needed to be corrected. He then put me on his knee and spanked me three times. I cried a lot, and I remember him putting me down and taking me into his arms and hugging me for a long time. He shed a few tears and told me he loved me. Despite all the crying and pain, I felt a weight lifted from my shoulders. All those months of hiding something I innately knew was wrong had finally been found out and dealt with. It released me from my guilt. That real-life lesson I had to learn the hard way exemplifies the heart of Hebrews 12:11: "No discipline seems pleasant at the time, but painful. Later on, however, it produces a harvest of righteousness and peace for those who have been trained by it."

I want to preface this chapter by saying that discipline is not just spanking. In fact, we rarely spanked our children when they were growing up. It only happened on serious occasions, like the incident above, when we saw that it was a continuous, rebellious heart attitude that needed to be dealt with. The majority of discipline that we administered to our children was loss of privileges and time-outs. We only spanked our children for four major things—lying, disrespect, fighting, and disobedience—and it was done between the ages of five and ten. If it's done too young, they won't understand it, and if it's done too old, they'll resent it. Between five and ten years old, they are the most receptive and moldable.

There are various forms of discipline. You can ask the Holy Spirit to lead you in what that means for you and your family. Discipline comes in all shapes and forms, even ways in which the parent doesn't have to get involved. For example, your child will learn really quickly without you having to say anything that putting his or her hand on the stove really, really hurts. Or that playing with scratch-and-sniff stickers at the bottom of the pool isn't such a good idea. They will figure out those kinds of things preeetty quickly. Then there are times you do have to get involved, like when your son or daughter chooses to play tag on an interstate freeway. You will say, "Yes, honey, you miraculously did not get hit by a semitruck today, but I am disciplining you now so that you don't get hit by one tomorrow!" There are other things in life that they will have to be corrected in because they might not necessarily feel the consequences now, but they will later. The main point of this chapter is not about *what* form of discipline is best, but about the overall importance of it in parenting.

Discipline, as we interpret it, is *painful consequences that show us that sin causes pain and separation from others and*

God, and it helps us turn our hearts back toward His path of righteousness.

If you are a father or mother, or if you hope to be one some-day, you must take to heart this message. Jon Courson, author and pastor, reveals four consequences that will inevitably occur if a parent never disciplines their child:

- frustration in the child
- consternation and division in the home
- exhaustion as a parent
- devastation in the nation and culture[1]

If a mom and a dad determine to never discipline, they're going to become exhausted, and the repercussions will affect not only the family, but our nation. Interestingly, in our generation, we are now seeing those repercussions. Did you know that the baby boomer generation started what became known as the most violent, anarchist, rebellious generation in American history? It continues to get worse through the millennial and Gen Z generations. One out of every thirty baby boomers will spend some time in prison. Something happened during that generation to get the ball rolling. That "something" was this: The baby boomer generation was the first in world history to be introduced to the concept that tra-ditional discipline is not relevant, needed, or even healthy. The person who introduced this was a man named Spock. Most of you are probably thinking of the *Star Trek* franchise that has a central character named Spock. You know, the smart guy with the elf ears and pointed eyebrows. Well, in this chapter, we're going to be talking about another man named Spock, but you're welcome to still picture Spock from *Star Trek* as you read.

The baby boomers' parents were influenced by a child authority named Dr. Benjamin Spock, who sold millions of books. That generation bought into Dr. Spock's theories[2] about parenting, and they continue to affect our culture to this day. His theories are based upon this idea: That little bundle of joy in your arms, that little baby, is inherently good, not a sinner. Man is innately and intrinsically good. Therefore, what you need to do is just let that good little baby mature and flower. Don't discipline. Discipline is unnecessary and primitive. Kids, according to Dr. Spock, are born good. Poor Dr. Spock, even with those long ears, he must not have been listening to the Word of God. The Bible says, "In sin did my mother conceive me" (Psalm 51:5 KJV). That means that at the moment of conception, I am a sinner. At the moment when my life began, there was a depraved sin nature that is part of me and part of every single person. From the very get-go, part of the human essence is sinful. I know that to be true. I raised twins! I never once taught my kids how to lie, be selfish, unforgiving, but they did those things. We all have. That is because the Bible says we are sinners. That we're *all* born sinners. "For all have sinned and fall short of the glory of God" (Romans 3:23). So Dr. Spock is lost in space as far as I'm concerned. He and others of like mind are wrong. We are still living with the repercussions of those teachings to this day.

The Bible, on the other hand, is not lost in space. It's down to earth. God might know a thing or two about how people function and how they're made. The book of Proverbs, a central hub for all sorts of wisdom, gives us sound advice about disciplining our children. Proverbs 13:24 (NLT) says, "Those who spare the rod of discipline hate their children. Those who love their children care enough to discipline them." If you don't correct and discipline your son or daughter, the Bible says that you're hating him or her. You are loving yourself more than you are loving them. You don't want to go through the emotional hassle or spend the energy. Instead of dealing with all the fuss, you would rather turn on the TV and not worry about it. That might be the easy way in the moment, but in the long run, it won't be good for your children.

Dos and Don'ts

If you are led by the Spirit to use spanking as a form of discipline for a very serious matter, make sure that you never use your hand. The hand is to be associated with affection and blessing. We never want our kids to have to guess whether they will get a pat on the head or a spank on the rear when they see our hands coming toward them. We want our hands to be linked with affection. There has to be a designated instrument you are to use to spank your child. Now, this is not giving you the green light to whack your kids based on your emotions—that's abuse and God is not okay with that. In Ephesians 6 it says, specifically to fathers, to not provoke your children to anger. Spanking is always to be measured and under the Spirit—that is, under control. When the time comes, it is your job to be in the Spirit, go get the proper instrument, and administer it in the proper way.

When disciplining your children, it's important to discipline immediately. Don't put it off. Don't say, "Wait till your dad gets home" or "If you do this one more time . . ." or "Okay, that's my last warning!" You need to deal with it right there, right then, immediately and consistently, but never with anger. Simply let your kids know that once that line is crossed, there will be discipline (time-outs, loss of privileges, and spanking—if you feel led by the Spirit in serious cases). If you love your son or daughter, you will discipline immediately and consistently.

Insights from Frank

Discipline is not a cookie cutter thing. Every child is different, and you are going to have to always pray and be led by the Spirit when you discipline your child. For some children, disciplining *all the time* can be counterproductive. If you see that they're getting more mad or so fearful of getting disciplined that they lie to you, then you have to break the cycle. Choose to give them grace and take them out for ice cream. Sometimes it's kindness and grace that leads people to repentance (see Romans 2:4). Dogmatic discipline is almost like legalism—it leads to rebelliousness. You have to humble yourself and always be in constant communication with the Holy Spirit about what you should do for each situation in regard to disciplining your child. Your pendulum needs to be balanced. Don't sway all the way to one side, where you never discipline your children, and don't sway all the way to the other side, where you are always disciplining your child. Choose your battles and ask the Holy Spirit to reveal to you the specific repeated strongholds that are occurring that need to be addressed with applied discipline. This is wisdom. This is Spirit-led discipline.

God is a good Father to us and knows exactly how we humans are made. So when He gives us instructions in His Word about child disciplining, we better get those highlighters out and start underlining and taking His instructions to heart. Proverbs 19:18 is one of those: "Discipline your children while there is hope. Otherwise you will ruin their lives" (NLT).

Without proper discipline, there will come a time when you'll look at your teenager or young adult and say, "It's hopeless. What went wrong?" Don't wait until that time. Do it now. (If you are a parent ready to put this book down because you just said that to yourself this morning—hold on. Jesus never gives up, and neither should you. Ask the Holy Spirit, the Helper, for guidance.) Kids desperately desire firm walls and boundaries to be in place and to be enforced. Why do I say this? Let's look at the story of Nehemiah in the Bible.

After Ezra, Zerubbabel, and Joshua (the high priest) led the children of Israel back to Jerusalem to rebuild the temple, the children of Israel still could not go back and freely worship. Why is that? Because the walls around the holy city were still in ruins. So Nehemiah took another group to go build the walls around the city so that worship could happen freely. The same is true for kids. They will have an easier time worshiping the Lord freely when walls are firmly established, when they know where the lines are and that those walls are immovable. Your children want you to be true and not succumb to tears. The most loving thing you can do for your kids, according to God, is to follow through—to be lovingly consistent and not back down. Let not your soul despair because of their crying.

Another instruction that God gives about disciplining your children is Proverbs 22:15. You can basically call God "butter" right now because He's on a roll with these instructions. Proverbs 22:15 says, "Folly is bound up in the heart of a child, but the rod of discipline will drive it far away."

Back in the 1990s there was a famous court case of two brothers who murdered their parents in cold blood. The trials stretched out for years with millions of dollars spent to keep the trials going. Ever since the Dr. Spock philosophy was introduced, it has been embraced by our culture that people are intrinsically good. So what about when they do something wrong, like the Menendez brothers, who went into their Beverly Hills home while Mom and Dad were watching TV, took out a shotgun, and shot Mom fifteen times and Dad seven times? Then got an inheritance of eighteen million dollars. They went out and bought Rolex watches, went to fancy restaurants, and took a trip to Europe. Denying, of course, that they were the killers. Finally, they confessed that they did it, but they wanted people to know that they were victims. They said that they were abused and had not been raised properly. They said that what they had done was not because they were bad but because they were sick.

Once a culture says people are good, then all of a sudden, when someone does something that is bad, it must be because they are sick. It is not because they are evil, or wicked, or murderers, or molesters, or killers. It is because they are sick. Now, when a person is sick with the flu or a cold, they're to be treated compassionately and nursed back to health with tenderness. Once culture starts saying that the root of the problem is that people are sick and not evil, the remedy becomes rehabilitation through education, not punishment. Like someone who went home with a bad case of the flu, the Menendez brothers went home with a bad case of "I'm mad at you" and blew their parents away. It's not sickness; it's sin. It's not a temporary ailment; it's wickedness and evil. Our culture today says, "We need to re-educate them. They're victims, they're sick." Once you get good at making excuses, that's all you'll be good for. It's illogical and dangerous. You are responsible for the decisions you make. You must not and cannot pin the blame on anyone else. The only kind of education that sinful behavior needs is the *board* of education being applied to the *seat* of learning (again, spanking is not the only form of discipline, I just really wanted to get that pun in there!). I'm not the one saying you need to discipline your children—it's what the Lord says. We are to drive out this foolishness, flush out this sin and rebellion with discipline and correction. We need to understand this, or our kids are going to have real problems.

Proverbs 23:13–14 says that our discipline actually keeps them from death. "Do not withhold discipline from a child; if you punish them with the rod, they will not die. Punish them with the rod and save them from death." Now, the word *death* can mean destruction, but other translations use the word "hell." The word "hell" here doesn't just mean the place of outer darkness—it means a person will be imprisoned if they are withheld discipline. If you feel another highlighter moment coming, your Spidey senses are indeed working.

Discipline has two effects that will keep the child from being imprisoned in their own soul. The first is that it releases the child from guilt. When we keep doing things we know are wrong and never get disciplined for it, the guilt builds up. We end up having people who willingly commit crimes just to be caught and rightly disciplined. The guilt becomes overwhelming and they cry out, "Catch me! Punish me!" (Just like good ol' Leo DiCaprio's character in the movie *Catch Me If You Can*.) When you discipline your children, there's a release of emotion and guilt. Their little hearts don't carry it anymore. Discipline causes pain, but it's healthy pain. When your child starts to go in a wrong direction, you apply that pressure and pain to bring them back on the right path. That's why God allows trials in our lives sometimes. It's painful, but it'll get us to snap back and make a U-turn. Loving means discipline.

Disciplining your children not only releases guilt, but the second point is that it *restores the relationship between the parent and the child.* When my daughter, Sarah, was disciplined, she didn't like it at the moment, but in the long run, she was thankful for the boundaries we set in place for her. I can tell you that there is a restoration that comes into the room when you apply biblical discipline, in contrast to what might be done in frustration. If you just say, "How could you do that?" or "What's wrong with you?" it doesn't help anything. It's when you are actually doing the disciplining—the crying takes place, the hugging follows—that there comes a *restoration* between the parent and the child. Remember King David in the Bible?

Well, he had a family that made high-drama soap operas look like a CSPAN segment about tax litigation. His kids were all messed up, and one of his sons, Amnon, ended up raping his own sister, Tamar, and David did nothing about it. The oldest son, Absalom, hated David for not dealing with Amnon for raping Tamar and eventually ended up leading a rebellion against his own father. That's why Solomon, David's son, wrote so much in the book of Proverbs about disciplining your children, because he saw firsthand what not disciplining your children will bring. If you want your kids to hate you, don't discipline or bring authority. The kids who end up hating their parents most often had no discipline growing up. The kids who had strong parameters and loving discipline, however, honored and loved their parents.

Insights from Sarah

"I can't believe it!" I said as I threw down my tennis racket. Scotty, my coach, was always getting on my case. It was in the middle of the blazing August summer heat, and we were once again training for the upcoming tennis season at the country club in Montclair, California. I was a junior in high school, and I was on the varsity tennis team for our school. Our tennis instructor at the country club, Scotty, would always make us do drills and practice techniques over and over again, but for some reason he always singled me out to practice and train harder. He kept pointing out my mistakes and would make me do the drills over again. I was at the point of pure frustration because none of the other girls were getting the same treatment, and they were messing up more than me. He kept calling my name, "Sarah! Stop getting caught in no-man's-land! Come to the net!" If anyone knows me, they know that I'm not the type to lose my temper, but I lost it. After practice, after the instructor had left and there were only a few teammates left packing up their gear, that's when I threw down my racket in frustration. I sat down in a heap and started to pick up my things. One of my teammates came up to me after seeing what had gone on during practice, and after seeing my overly dramatic scene. She sat down and told me, "Sarah, I can clearly see that you're frustrated with the way Scotty keeps calling you out. But look at it this way, at least he's focusing on you. He doesn't even remember my name half of the time." I realized right then what my teammate was saying. At least Scotty knew who I was, and he cared enough about me or saw some kind of potential in me so that he wanted to work with me, to correct my mistakes and make me better.

Looking back, I am so thankful that my mom and dad cared enough to discipline me. Intuitively, I knew that it wasn't at all easy for them to discipline me. But it showed me that they loved and cared so much for me. They didn't want me to go down a destructive road with no discipline. They saw great potential in me and wanted to release me of guilt and correct those mistakes, just like good ol' Coach Scotty.

Our heavenly Father, who is the ultimate model of a how-to parent, disciplines us (His children) for our good and because He loves us. Hebrews 12:5–8 says,

> My son, do not make light of the Lord's discipline, and do not lose heart when he rebukes you, because the Lord disciplines the one he loves, and he chastens everyone he accepts as his son. Endure hardship as discipline; God is treating you as his children. For what children are not disciplined by their father? If you are not disciplined—and everyone undergoes discipline—then you are not legitimate, not true sons and daughters at all.

You might question the trials and discipline you are facing, just as I questioned Coach Scotty's persistent correction, but remember—the Lord disciplines those He loves. The verse continues with, "God disciplines us for our good, in order that we may share in his holiness" (verse 10). Discipline might seem hard at the moment, but remember that it will be for their good. And your kids, in the long run, will thank you for caring enough for them—just like I am eternally grateful for my parents' discipline.

We can see this at work with the way our heavenly Father disciplines us, His children. Proverbs 3:12 (NKJV) says, "Whom the LORD loves He corrects." His discipline may be to cleanse you of sin, stretch your faith, or build your character. Whatever His goal is, you can be sure of this one thing: It is out of love, not anger. In fact, He really does see potential in you that He wishes to develop. That development requires discipline. Therefore, the discipline that we experience from our heavenly Father is actually favor, not wrath. And the same is true with parents. If we love our children, we will discipline them. But the discipline should never come from a place of anger. We see the great potential our kids can have, and we want them to walk in all that God has for them. Just like our heavenly Father tells us the reason behind the discipline in His Word, so should we as parents tell our kids that our discipline comes from love and favor toward them. And just like Sarah's tennis story, it will change their whole perspective.

Always Explain Why

The book of Proverbs gives us one more little gem about discipline, and it's found in Proverbs 29:15 (NKJV): "The rod and rebuke give wisdom, but a child left to himself brings shame to his mother." It's the rod *and* rebuke that give wisdom, not the rod *or* rebuke. There's a need for painful consequences (discipline) with our kids, and there is also the need for a verbal, intellectual, and spiritual interaction. You need them both. That means you only discipline your children if there's also going to be a verbal, intellectual, and spiritual interaction. You have to explain why you're doing what you're doing. You're not just venting your frustration when you discipline your children. Discipline releases the guilt and brings the parent and child together. The rebuke explains "the why." For instance, lying is wrong because of how it brings repercussions like mistrust and bad decisions.

Do you want your son or daughter to walk wisely? The rod and rebuke together (painful consequences and intellectual interaction) will bring your son or daughter wisdom. Don't take it personally—it's not. They are sinful; that's just how they are. And we are here to show them love, kindness, and self-control. It is key that they know why they are getting disciplined so that it will not provoke anger in their hearts.

Most importantly, you need to make sure you are not angry while disciplining. Take a step back and count to ten. Splash water on your face, take deep breaths, or go to another room to pray. In other words, make sure to put *yourself* on a time-out to relax if you need it. Then, go discipline. Then you say to your child, "Do you know what you did wrong?" "Next time, are we going to do it differently?" Let them know they are not sinning against you, but against God. Show him or her the cross and what Jesus had to go through because of our sin. Teach them the fear of the Lord so that they won't want to do anything that displeases the Lord.

Discipline should always happen within the context of fellowship and a healthy relationship with your children. That way, when you discipline them, they know it's coming out of love and that you have their best interest in mind. When your bond with them is strong, they won't view your discipline with frustration, but will understand that you love them and want to save them from the things in them that will destroy them if left unchecked. It all comes down to fostering that healthy relationship with your kids first. A healthy relationship is fostered by spending time with them, giving them your full attention, engaging in conversation with them about things that interest them, controlling your emotions, and giving them verbal affirmation.

Let me be honest with you. At this season in my life (my kids are now adults), I can look back and see that I have not been a perfect parent. Not at all. But I have understood that these are nonnegotiable principles: discipline and verbal correction. Godly parenting is not about being perfect. Instead, it's about being consistent—consistency in applying God's instructions on how to discipline your children. Don't let your own guilt about not being a better parent stop you. Repair your mistakes by apologizing and forgiving yourself. Then discipline them, interact with them. You tell them not only *what* but *why*. I can look back now, and I can tell you that it works. Neither my son nor my daughter is perfect, but they are godly and walking with the Lord wholeheartedly. By God's grace, they have never veered off or rebelled against the Lord. I say all this not because my husband and I are wonderful, but because God's instructions are wonderful. They work. As a result, I am beyond proud of my children.

PUT IT INTO PRACTICE:
DISCIPLINE

- Meditate on these verses in God's Word that reference discipline.
  1. Hebrews 12:11: "No discipline seems pleasant at the time, but painful. Later on, however, it produces a harvest of righteousness and peace for those who have been trained by it."
  2. Proverbs 13:24: "Whoever spares the rod hates their children, but the one who loves their children is careful to discipline them."
  3. Proverbs 19:18: "Discipline your children while there is hope. Otherwise you will ruin their lives" (NLT).

4. Proverbs 22:15: "Folly is bound up in the heart of a child, but the rod of discipline will drive it far away."

5. Proverbs 23:13–14: "Do not withhold discipline from a child; if you punish them with the rod, they will not die. Punish them with the rod and save them from death."

6. Proverbs 3:12: "Whom the LORD loves He corrects" (NKJV).

7. Proverbs 29:15: "The rod and rebuke give wisdom, but a child left to himself brings shame to his mother" (NKJV).

- Talk with your spouse about how he or she disciplines, and make sure you are on the same page, that the two of you agree with the things you will discipline for—like our four major things (lying, disrespect, intentional harm to others, and disobedience).

- If you choose to spank, follow this process: Send the child to his or her room, approach the child lovingly and explain why, do not use your hand, be in the Spirit and under control, spank no more than three times and with a force only strong enough to sting but not harm or bruise, hug and love with the goal of restoration. Remember our advice about the age range for spanking: ages five to ten, and only for serious offenses.

- Administer other forms of discipline, especially in pre-teens and teens, such as loss of privileges (no phone, no car, grounding, extra chores).

- Ask the Holy Spirit within you to give grace and mercy and timing in your discipline. Your focus should always be Spirit-led when it comes to discipline and always in the context of a healthy relationship with your child.

PART FIVE

SPIRITUAL GROWTH AND PRACTICAL PARENTING

12

HOLY SPIRIT–LED PARENTING

The Parenting Game-Changer

As Christians, aren't you so grateful that you no longer live under the law but under the new covenant of grace? Instead of animal sacrifices and trying to abide by the law, we now have Jesus' ultimate sacrifice on the cross. When we believe in Him, His righteousness is imputed upon us, His Holy Spirit comes inside of us, and His law is now written on our hearts. It's a whole new way of living—hallelujah! What if I told you that this same concept can be applied to parenting and it will be the key that will safeguard your kids from rebelling? You'd probably say, "Sign me up!" Good news: Through the guidance of the Word, my husband and I did apply Spirit-led parenting to our kids, and it was a game-changer (especially in their teenage years).

When we look at the Old Testament, we see that the Law only brought consternation, repeated failure, and rebellion. Constant rules and regulations didn't work—they just made the rebellion from those rules more pronounced and the guilt of failure even worse. So the answer, as explained in Romans 7, is not to put yourself under the law but to reckon yourself dead to the law, because the law will produce in you fleshly activity. You may be asking, "What do you mean by that, Mary?" I'll tell you what I mean: *Regulations that are imposed in a legalistic manner will always produce rebellion.* The proverbial PK (pastor's kid) illustrates this perfectly. I know this firsthand. My husband is a pastor, so my son and daughter grew up as PKs. Pastor's kids are often associated with rebellion, and for good reason. If you've been around church for very long, you've seen it: They do their own thing, sneak behind the church and vape, walk away from the faith, et cetera. Why is that? Because the well-meaning pastor tells his kids that they're not going to embarrass him or his church, so they're not going to do this, this, or this. "You're my children and I'm a preacher, so you're going to get in line." And what happens is that the kids, under obligations, rules, and the law, become rebellious. If we put obligations, rules, and laws on people, they will ultimately veer off into rebellion. So what's the answer? The answer is to send the law away. Don't put people under regulations or rules. Instead, teach them about the new covenant, which is *grace*. The new covenant looks like this: The Lord is working with your children; He's writing His will upon the tablets of their hearts and giving direction (see Jeremiah 31:33); He's causing them to see what they should do, and that it's not a "got to" but a "get to." Isn't that so much more beautiful than rules, regulations, and legalism? It's a whole new way of living. Here's how my husband and I implemented it when parenting our son and daughter.

Throughout their formative years (ages one through ten) we laid down boundaries for them, but once they made their faith their own and we could see the Holy Spirit working in them (which was about the start of their junior high years), we started to apply Spirit-led parenting. When you look at your own spiritual walk with the Lord, you know there are certain things that God puts on your heart. When I became saved at eighteen years old, and the Holy Spirit came inside of me and wrote His laws on my heart, I started to walk differently. When everyone else was going out partying and drinking, the Holy Spirit put it on my heart to no longer partake in those activities. It wasn't a legalistic church rule that I had to follow, but simply what the Holy Spirit was communicating to me. My husband and I applied the same Spirit-led parenting to our children when they came of age. When it came time for them to go to dances, I would say, "Here's my opinion on that. I believe that oftentimes at those dances a lot of mischief and temptations can take place, like sensual dancing, drinking, and boys trying to hook up with girls. I know what takes place because I was once your age. So the thing that you need to do now is pray about what the Lord wants you to do. Is that a place where you can be a vibrant witness for the Lord, or is it a place where the atmosphere would be a grief to the Holy Spirit within you and put you into dangerous or tempting situations?" Then I had them pray about it. I didn't make a dictatorial decree and say, "I declare, thou shall not venture unto the dance henceforth!" Tempting as it may be to lay down the law in this way, this is not Spirit-led parenting. After I had made clear my opinion and told them to take it to the Lord, I would say, "If the Lord gives you a green light—then God bless you. If you think you can be a witness there, then you have my blessing and my backing. But if you know that it's going to be an atmosphere that's not the best for you, then I would say don't do it."

This set my kids on a track to become adults who pray about decisions and are Spirit-led. My husband and I did not tell our kids that we don't go to dances because it's against our religion or because we're a pastor's family. We simply told them to pray to the Lord and ask Him what He thought was best. In the end, my kids almost always came to us and said that the Lord was leading them not to go to the dance or not to go see a certain movie that everyone else was seeing. This Spirit-led parenting safeguarded them from rebelling. It set them up to have an intimate relationship with the Lord, and they grew confident in their convictions and in wisdom.

Insights from Frank

A parent's aim is to foster a house of both truth and grace. This means that parents should constantly be speaking the truth of God's Word and adding a tremendous amount of grace by not putting pressure on their kids and demanding perfection. Combining discipline with grace also showcases to your kids the picture of God's salvation. Discipline models the cross by showing them that the price has been paid and they're forgiven. Grace models God's goodness that leads people to forgiveness. For example, Sarah had a tendency to lie and be sneaky when she was little. I started to notice that whenever she would lie, it wasn't just to lie for lying's sake, but she was afraid of getting spanked for what she did. I prayed and asked the Holy Spirit to guide me, and He told me to break the cycle by giving her mercy and grace. So when the situation occurred again, instead of disciplining her, I told her what she did was wrong, but that I was going to show her grace and mercy and take her out for ice cream. That did the trick. And we never really had a real problem with lying again in her formative years. The Holy Spirit so gently reminded me that it doesn't always have to be discipline, but sometimes goodness that leads to repentance. This is a perfect example of Spirit-led parenting resulting in heart change.

The new covenant is also incorporating identity into their decision-making. Kids will make choices based on their identity, so let them know what their identity is in Christ. One key lesson we learned in parenting is this: We didn't tell our kids what to do—we told them who they are.

For instance, instead of saying "Don't get drunk at a party!" Or "Don't watch pornography!" tell your kids who they are in Christ. That they are the righteousness of God in Christ Jesus. That they are not drunk with wine but filled with the Spirit. That they are vessels of honor and purity and that this identity makes them set no unclean thing before their eyes.

My daughter once asked her very healthy friend how he's able to eat clean and stay fit, and he told her that he took the verse in 1 Corinthians 6 that says your body is a temple of the Holy Spirit as his identity and it made it easier for him to say no to unhealthy food. When a waiter would offer him an unhealthy dessert at the end of a meal, he would say, "I don't do unhealthy desserts. That's not who I am." It was easier for him to resist temptation and make good choices because he knew his identity.

That's the new covenant. The new covenant is grace, a new identity, and letting the Spirit lead. All we should want as parents is to teach our kids to walk in the Spirit and know their identity. No regulations. You simply do what the Lord is telling you to do. That's where the real victory in parenting will be. No rules that lead to rebellion, legalism, or a fleshly reaction. Help your kids open up their hearts to the Lord and then be obedient to Him. That's the new covenant. That's the new way of parenting.

Have this hope: As you continue to faithfully and consistently raise your kids up in the Lord, eventually they are going to make their faith their own, they'll have their own revelation of and encounter with God. Everything will change. Reading the Bible won't be an obligation but adoration. They'll be convicted by the Holy Spirit; they'll choose to turn away from evil and pursue holiness. So take heart. Stay consistent. Stay Spirit-led. God will do the rest.

Parent like the Father

Ever heard the saying, "Father knows best"? Well, the same can be applied to how our heavenly Father parents His children (the bride of Christ—the Church). All the way back in the beginning of Genesis, we see God's first and probably most important component of parenting—boundaries. God gave Adam and Eve boundaries in the garden. They were to eat freely from any tree in the garden except the fruit from the Tree of the Knowledge of Good and Evil, for God told them that if they ate of it they would certainly die (see Genesis 2:16–17). What we see here is that God gave man three very important things: freedom, choice, and consequence. He gave them the freedom to eat freely from the garden. He gave them the choice to obey or not obey His only command. He also gave them a consequence if they were to disobey. Freedom, choice, and consequence are all so very powerful when applied to boundaries in parenting. If God our heavenly Father used them, we probably should take a hint and use them too.

In parenting, we need to let our kids know that people want to have boundaries. If they had total freedom, it might be fun for a moment, but it would leave them anxious and empty. Children want boundaries and structure. It gives them purpose and goals in life. The difficulty for most parents is that they want to raise independent kids but are tempted to fall into helicopter parenting.

Freedom, Choice, Consequence (FCC)

Author and speaker Chip Judd is an amazing communicator on developing healthy relationships, and he is the originator of applying freedom, choice, and consequences (FCC) in modern-day parenting. There are three general developmental stages that he says are essential in parenting and in almost any growing relationship.

1. Direct Control/Dependence: ages 0–12
2. Indirect Control/Independence: ages 13–21
3. No Control/Interdependence: ages 21 and onward[1]

Direct Control/Dependence: 0–12

This is the stage when your kids' safety and development are your sole responsibility. This stage is called dependence because your kids are utterly dependent upon you for everything they need. This generally lasts until about age twelve.

Indirect Control/Independence: 13–21

This is when a child begins to enter adolescence, and changes start to happen physiologically. The focus/dependence shifts from parents to peers. This is when you have to adjust your parenting. This stage is called independence because your goal during this stage is to incrementally give your child more and more responsibility for managing his or her life. In this stage, they begin to figure out their identity and long-term goals.

No Control/Interdependence: 21–

This is the launching stage of life and when you see your goal of a human being who doesn't need you all the time. They go to God for advice, and they're not asking you to borrow money or pay their phone bill. They need to be mastering those responsibilities in this stage. This is the stage when your children can come to you and ask for your help if they want it.

As a parent, you give your children appropriate freedom for each developmental stage. Within that freedom, they make good or bad choices. If they make a bad choice, your job is to make sure they experience a consequence that fits.

Insights from Sarah

One of the ways my parents practiced freedom, choice, and consequences was they gave us the freedom to get whatever grades we wanted. However, if we chose to get good grades, they would reward us. They told us that we were smart and could achieve anything we put our minds to. With that, they showed us what freedom looked like, and that our choices can give us positive consequences. This internalized in us a steadfast character of taking responsibility.

If a child's behavior is bad, they need to experience a consequence that fits. If you, as a parent, are protecting them from the consequence of the choice they made, you are harming them in the long run. This is what we're seeing right now in America. In certain areas, shoplifting by homeless people is not a crime, and first-degree murderers are let out early, along with rapists and pedophiles. When people are protected from the consequences of their decisions, that will only lead to destruction and demise. This is why FCC is so crucial and pivotal in raising children.

Here are a couple of practical, age-appropriate examples.

FCC Toddler Example: Your child doesn't want to brush their teeth. Instead of forcing them to do it, give them a choice: "Okay, you don't have to brush your teeth, but that means you can't have candy tomorrow because candy gives you cavities, especially if you don't brush your teeth. So you choose—brush your teeth and you can have candy tomorrow, or don't brush your teeth and you can't have candy tomorrow. The choice is yours." Most likely, they will choose to brush their teeth. Giving them a small choice like that (and a sense of consequence to their choice) is empowering to them. This applies so well to parenting a strong-willed child. Strong-willed children need options. They throw temper tantrums if they feel like their choices are being taken away. So give them choices and let them choose what the consequence (good or bad) will be.

FCC Teenager Example: Your teenage son wants to hang out with his guy friends on a Saturday night. You want him back by ten, and you explain that if he's not home by then, he will experience the consequences of that choice. If he ends up coming back at midnight, you have to make it clear that his choice to come home late will result in a negative consequence. How you handle this situation is going to make a big impression on your child. Remember, boundaries in parenting produce *security* in your child. If you're itching to take that highlighter out, this is your moment right here. Chip Judd says it best: "Discipline is the art of teaching a child self-control by managing their consequences."[2] This is the same discipline our loving heavenly Father uses to teach us. He manages our physical, relational, and emotional long-lasting consequences to teach us self-control. Thus, disciplining this way is at its very essence parenting like the Father.

There's a powerful reason why God gave humans free will and choice. There's a reason why He put the Tree of Knowledge of Good and Evil in the middle of the garden with Adam and Eve. He did it because He knew that without choice, real love wouldn't exist. If God created us all like robots, where He could simply wind us up like a toy and we would say, "I love You, God. I love You, God," that wouldn't be real love. A true response to His love is to choose to say no to the world and to make Jesus the Lord of our lives. The same goes for parenting. When we parent with forced obedience, we're just instilling fear in our kids and not letting them develop the character to make responsible decisions. Instead of always trying to be in control, give them the freedom to make choices that will result in certain consequences (good or bad).

It will be incredibly beneficial for the parent to pick their battles and realize their children need this sense of positive power every single day. They need to feel like they have some sense of control, that they're not just constantly being told what to do and how to live their lives. I have had friends go into deep depression because they had parents who did just that—told them how to live their lives. They told them, "You have to go into this occupation because that's what we've always done." It went against how they were wired.

One important thing to note is that teens have an underdeveloped orbitofrontal cortex—the area of the brain that weighs the consequences of potential decisions before undertaking those choices. This is why so many of the bad choices you made in your life were as a teenager, because that part of your brain was not fully developed yet. This makes it all the more important for parents to guide and "brain train" their kids to look at the long-term effects of every choice they make. The Bible knew this about teens' brains, which is why Proverbs 22:6 is so important. "Train up a child in the way he should go, and when he is old he will not depart from it" (NKJV). It doesn't mean they won't make silly choices as teenagers, but if you help raise them up in the Word and with godly fear, they will come to the point of deciding to follow God for themselves when they are older. Also, let us not miss a key nugget at the beginning: "the way he should go" could be translated from the Hebrew as "in his own way." This means that raising children isn't just mechanical, like training animals. But rather, as we depend on the Holy Spirit, it's important that we learn how God would have us teach each child individually.

This is the end goal in parenting: You are preparing your child to walk in the fear of the Lord and submit to His will. It's all about preparation. You want to prepare them to develop healthy relationship boundaries. You want to prepare them to be responsible. You want to prepare them to use wisdom in weighing the consequences in every situation, choosing right while experiencing freedom. These are the boundaries that God created man to thrive in and live safely in. Freedom, choice, and consequence might seem like three simple steps, but they won't be easy to apply. You have to be firm and pleasantly persistent. But if you parent and discipline like the Father, you can never go wrong.

PUT IT INTO PRACTICE:
SPIRIT-LED PARENTING AND FCC

- Apply Spirit-led parenting by cultivating the relationship your children have with the Lord and having them go to the Father for direction and guidance. Cultivate their relationship with the Lord by giving them tips on how to read their Bible (regularly, with pen in hand—we will go into this further in the next chapter), showing them how to pray and naturally talk to God (like you would a friend), and showing them how to hear the Father's voice and know when God is talking (you have peace, it lines up with the Bible). Remember, Spirit-led parenting is teaching your kids how to think, pray, and be led by the Spirit.

- Are there persistent issues you are facing with your children? Before the offense occurs again, ask the Holy Spirit how you can incorporate freedom, choice, and consequences so you're ready to parent like the Father next time.

13

THE SECRET SAUCE

Equipping Your Family with the Word,
Worship, and Prayer

Have you ever had a secret sauce or ingredient in a recipe that totally transformed your dish and everyone craved to know what it was that made it so good? I'm woman enough to admit that the real cook in our family is my husband. Our family's favorite dish is his famous breakfast egg burritos. He has a secret ingredient that makes those puppies drip goodness with every bite. There was only one time that he didn't add his secret ingredient because we were out of it, and those egg burritos just weren't the same. It was indeed what transformed those egg blanket babies into a culinary feast.

In our spiritual lives, there are three "secret" ingredients that will transform our parenting: the Word of God, worship, and prayer. This is the dynamite that opens up the roads for God to work in our children's lives. God gives us a manual, His Word, to raise up children in the Lord. We also have to keep in mind that every child is different and the enemy will work overtime to try to get them to fall. There is also the matter of free will. Look at Adam and Eve, they had the most perfect parent—God the Father! And yet, they still chose to disobey and ended up falling. This is why the Word, worship, and prayer are so important. The Word will be implanted in their hearts and it won't return void, worship will bind up the works of the enemy over your children's lives, and prayer will loose the Holy Spirit to work in their hearts and in their minds. Parents, especially those who are raising teenagers, will need the Word, worship, and prayer as their lifeline to get through those years. No question about it.

Here's the thing: Everybody's going to make their own choice about what they're going to do with their lives, and there's nothing you can do to change that. It's good to try to tell your kids what's right, but you have to be careful that they don't feel like every time they come near you, you're preaching to them or constantly finding something wrong with them. So it takes a lot of prayer and a lot of God showing you timing, so you know when to just pray and let it go and when to address it. I remember there were some concerns that I had for my children, but we kept praying for them, kept surrounding them with the Word and worship, and continued to be good examples, and both of them turned out great. They are both walking with the Lord, serving God, walking in their calling, and raising up disciples. Yes, they did have struggles and had to learn some lessons the hard way. But rest assured, it will work itself out in the end if you continue to trust God and pray for them. If you are doing your best to raise them up in the Lord—serving God together, saturating your lives with the Word of God, discipling them— those things will not return void. Through your constant prayer and intercession, God will always bring them back.

Raising kids, especially in today's age, is extremely challenging. There's so much more immorality now than when I was raising my kids. They weren't dealing with the temptations that kids are dealing with today. But I really believe the most important thing about raising a child is not so much what you tell them to do, but what they see you do. What kind of home atmosphere do you have? Is it filled with visible praise and trust in God? Are you looking for ways to sincerely praise your children? And what kind of a home life are they living in? Are you doing things as a family, or is everybody going in different directions all the time because they're just so busy? If you provide that right atmosphere, and you give your children the Word, worship, and prayer, that will be the secret sauce that will transform your parenting.

Secret Sauce Ingredient Number One: the Word

If you have not read Psalm 119, take a break from this book and go read it. The main theme of the psalm is the benefits and the blessings of being in the Bible. If you will be a person of the Book, you will be blessed in every area of your life. Psalm 119 can be summed up by Joshua 1:8: "This Book of the Law shall not depart from your mouth, but you shall meditate in it day and night, that you may observe to do according to all that is written in it. For then you will make your way prosperous, and then you will have good success" (NKJV). That's what Psalm 119 tells us over and over throughout the chapter. Job was one of the most successful and prosperous people that ever walked the face of the earth, and he had this to say: "I have not departed from the commands of his lips; I have treasured the words of his mouth more than my daily bread" (Job 23:12). Wow. In other words, Job is saying that if it comes to a choice between eating food or being in the Word, he would opt for the Word. He would choose the Bible over breakfast, Luke over lunch, and Daniel over dinner. This was Job's heart, and God blessed him for that.

This is key to a prosperous life and a God-fearing family: Love the Word. Parents, be an example to your kids and be in the Word daily. Talk about it with your kids while you're eating your meals, driving in the car, shopping at the grocery store. Let it always be on your lips. And, most importantly, teach your kids to love the Word. Model to them that when you read the Bible, it is not out of obligation but out of adoration—for when you love the Word, you're loving Jesus. Encourage your children to write their favorite verses on note cards and fill their rooms with them. Have contests about who can memorize the most verses. Make it fun. The Word of God will not return void—it will come back to their remembrance when they need it most. Teach them to study the Word from cover to cover and to ask questions. Here are some helpful tips to guide your kids.

How to read your Bible

Read consistently. Teach your kids to read the Bible daily, even if they do not understand it. The Word of God will not return void. Eventually, a passage that they've read over and over will finally click and they will have a revelation. That's the way the Word works. It is living and active, sharper than any double-edged sword (Hebrews 4:12). It's the only book that will read you. Take, for example, Genesis 5. If you've ever read that chapter, you've probably breezed over it, thinking it was just a boring genealogy list from Adam to Noah. But did you know that if you were to take the English root from ten of the earliest Hebrew names mentioned in the Bible, from Adam (which means "man") through Noah (which means "rest"), it would spell out the Gospel? The meanings of those words put together give us "Man (is) appointed mortal sorrow; (but) the Blessed God shall come down teaching (that) His death shall bring (the) despairing rest." Doesn't that just put a lump in your throat? Chuck Missler, who first discovered this, wrote, "In the earliest chapters of the book of Genesis, God had already laid out His plan of redemption for the predicament of mankind. It is the beginning of a love story, ultimately written in blood on the wooden cross . . . erected in Judea almost two thousand years ago."[1] This is why it's so important to teach your kids to read and study consistently. There are treasures like this just waiting to be found.

Read expectantly. When they're at an appropriate age to read and write, have them do their daily Bible readings with a pen and paper or a journal. When we come expecting that the Lord is going to speak, we make sure that we have something to write it down with. Show your kids that the Word is like a map to hidden treasure. Each time they open it and write it out, they are enriching their souls.

Read conversationally. Show your kids that reading the Bible doesn't have to be boring but like an exciting conversation with your best friend. Have them read a passage in the Bible and talk to God out loud or in their minds and ask Him what He means by that, or how it can be applied to their lives. Even converse with God about how crazy awesome that verse was and praise Him for it. This will make reading the Bible part of our personal, intimate relationship with Jesus.

Read obediently. Simply put, our Lord is so awesomely kind to us that He does not pile instruction and revelation on top of us; instead, He gives us one thing to do at a time. If your kids come to you and say, "I'm not getting anything out of my Bible reading," ask them, "Have you done that last thing that God has told you to do? Try that first. Maybe He's waiting to give you more instruction and revelation until you have been obedient to what He's already told you." This is a call to teach our children to be doers of the Word.

Secret Sauce Ingredient Number Two: Prayer

Prayer works, plain and simple. Saturate your kids' lives with prayer. Just prayer alone will take your parenting to a whole new level. One single prayer can do more in one second than a lifetime of trying to convince somebody to do what's right.

My husband and I prayed together for our children every morning, we prayed with them before they went to school in the morning, and we prayed with them every night before they went to bed. We would take their weaknesses throughout the day (for example, if they were hyperactive) and pray out loud at night that the Lord would take that zeal and use it for His good. We would take the negatives and turn them into positives by speaking life over them at night. We had devotions every Saturday morning and would pray and take Communion together. Often, my husband and I would go to our prayer closets (or any place inside or outside where we could be alone), get on our knees, and intercede on behalf of our kids. I would send quick prayers to God for them while I was driving and running errands. I would pray for them whenever I sensed something was wrong that they weren't telling me, and I would pray for them when they were misbehaving or having a fleshly attitude. Prayer is so important in parenting, because my husband and I are only human and, well, God is God! He can do infinitely more than we can do, and if it's impossible with man, it's possible with God. He knows the past, present, and future, and He knows exactly how you should raise your kids. Go to Him for wisdom. Go to Him even to just get out a good venting. He's always listening and always willing and able to intercede on our behalf. All we have to do is humble ourselves and pray.

Insights from Sarah

I can honestly say that my parents' prayer over me transformed my life. My parents prayed for my salvation, they prayed for protection and guidance, they prayed that the Holy Spirit would convict me if I was wrong. I remember so many instances in my life (especially in my teenage years) when I would be in a bad mood and have a wrong attitude about a situation. I remember my mom would tell me to go to my room and pray to the Lord. At first, in my pride, I wouldn't pray but just sit alone and pout. Eventually, I felt a stirring in my heart that was leading me to surrender and pray. I would ask God for forgiveness and go downstairs and apologize to my parents. In every instance, I later found out that my mom had been praying that the Holy Spirit would convict me and help me. In her wisdom, she knew that all her words wouldn't get to my heart, but the Holy Spirit could. My mom is a prayer warrior, and I can attest to the fact that I am the woman that I am today because of her radical and consistent prayers over me. Prayer not only transformed my life, but it also bonded us together. We take prayer walks every so often in the morning together and share what's on our hearts. We pray and do spiritual battle together. So if you want to be close to your children, and be victorious in the spiritual battle at the same time, pray with and for your kids.

Pray for encounters

Pray that your kids will have an encounter with God, like Jacob. Jacob was a deceiver and a manipulator until he had an encounter with God and wrestled with Him. That one encounter brought him to his knees, and God changed his name to Israel, which means "governed by God." Once they have an encounter with the presence of God, nothing can pull them away. It's okay if they have to go through a trial—that's often what gets their attention and pushes them closer to God. Develop atmospheres where they can experience the presence of God—worship together in the car, take them to worship conferences, have them pray over someone to get healed, and take them on mission trips.

Teaching prayer and spiritual warfare

If you've ever wondered if you should talk to your children about spiritual warfare, the answer is a big *yes*! When your kids are aware that there is a battle going on all around them, they'll see the absolute necessity of putting on the full armor of God daily. The enemy's greatest trick is to convince people that he doesn't exist. He doesn't want people to know that he's constantly trying to attack, deceive, kill, and destroy our lives. Many times, parents think the enemy will not go after their kids because they are young—but he does. In fact, he loves to go after kids when they're young because if he can get them to start a negative thought pattern or habitual sin early, it will be even harder for them to break free. When children are being attacked by the enemy—such as when they have nightmares, temptations, negative thoughts, fears—they are not aware it's spiritual warfare. Yes, our Lord does protect them as we pray daily for them, but it helps to teach them to be ready and equipped.

My husband and I taught our children early that there are two different forces out there in the spiritual realm—the light and the dark. We taught them that God's army is always the strongest: "Greater is He who is in you than he who is in the world" (1 John 4:4 NASB). And we also taught them that they need *not* be afraid but stand next to Jesus by calling out His name, and the evil forces will always flee. Teach your kids Psalm 91, and about the armor of God in Ephesians 6. I always told my children that we get dressed with the armor of God spiritually the same way we get dressed in the morning. Our children need to stand firm against the enemy and the powers that attack not only them, but our families, their friends, and spiritual brothers and sisters. Teach your children how to pray against the attacks of the enemy. Teach them that sometimes the enemy's attacks are direct and sometimes they are subtle (2 Corinthians 11:14–15). Teach them also the difference between the good and the bad, dark and light. Here are a few examples of the enemy's strategies: lies, strongholds in the mind, fear, gossip, idolizing oneself, pride, and jealousy to steal, kill, and destroy. But Jesus came that you might have life through truth, forgiveness, dying to yourself, humility, and the gifts of the Spirit.

If you signed up to be in the military and you were assigned to go overseas to fight, the military would most likely teach you how to fight in hand-to-hand combat and how to use a firearm. They teach you this so that you can be prepared and ready for battle.

The same goes with equipping our children with the knowledge and the resources to fight in this spiritual war. It comes down to two things: showing them how to fight with the Word of God and showing them how to put on the full armor of God. The enemy is very good at telling lies and saying the opposite of the truth of God. When the enemy attacks with lies in our thoughts, we must teach our children how to use the truth of the Word to fight back. Jesus shows us the way in Matthew 4:1–11, when the enemy (Satan) came to tempt Him. Every word the enemy said to Jesus was to try to make Him fall, but Jesus repeatedly said, "It is written," and came back with truth to fight the lies. This is why it's so important to saturate our children with the Word of God. Have them memorize certain verses that pertain to whatever they're struggling with. Have them post those verses around their rooms. Speak the Word whenever you're around them. Teach them how to take those verses that they hid in their hearts and declare them out loud whenever the enemy attacks. We need to know the Word and use the Word in spiritual battle in order to fight back and be victorious. We conquer the enemy by the truth of God's Word. This is so vital to teach our children and to apply to our own lives (remember, you do it, then you teach it).

The one offensive weapon we have is the sword of the Spirit, which is the Word of God. Now, we must teach our children how to put on the full armor of God. In Ephesians 6:10–18, Paul emphasizes that putting on the full armor is necessary if we are to defeat Satan. The area in our life that we leave unguarded is sure to be the very place that Satan attacks. That's why it's important to put on the *full* armor. Here is a brief summary of what each piece of the armor is and how to apply it.

The belt of truth. This is the part of the armor that holds everything else together. Your protection against temptation and doubt starts with knowing God's truth. This also calls us to live a life that's free of lying and hidden sin.

The breastplate of righteousness. The breastplate covers your heart. It protects the areas where you're most vulnerable to temptation. We should also always rely on the purity, or righteousness, of Jesus and strive to be like Him.

The shoes of the Gospel of peace. Allow God to guide your feet by following His calling in your life.

The shield of faith. If you ask the Lord to strengthen your faith, this verse says that it will become strong enough to act as a shield from the enemy's attacks.

The helmet of salvation. Once you accept Jesus as your Savior, you are forgiven from your sins and receive eternal life. Colossians 3:2 also advises believers to keep their thoughts on heavenly pursuits: "Set your minds on things above, not on earthly things."

The sword of the Spirit. If you familiarize yourself with the Bible, you can quote it to overcome the temptation to sin, just like Jesus did. You can also use it to pray and to renew your mind.

And last but not least, pray in the Spirit. We put on the armor by means of prayer, and we pray by means of the Holy Spirit. It is very important to teach our children to pray and keep praying and not lose heart (see Luke 18:1–5) and to "pray without ceasing" (1 Thessalonians 5:17 NKJV). This does not mean we go around reciting prayers all day long, but that whenever we are being attacked by the enemy, we ought to pray. Prayer involves worship, adoration, confession of sin, supplication, and thanksgiving. We should not just ask for things when we pray, but intercede for others, fighting in the Spirit through prayer and praise. This is the way we defeat the enemy! As the Mandalorians say, "This is the way." Or, as the theme of this book says, "This is the *Jesus* way."

Secret Sauce Ingredient Number Three: Worship

At eighteen years old, my life had been a series of tumultuous events. When I lost all hope, God literally stepped in and saved me from taking my life. Soon after that crazy experience, I approached one of the teachers at my school who was a Christian and asked if I could go to her church with her. We went that very Sunday, and I have to admit, it was so very different from the Catholic church. They played actual live band music. It was the first time in my life I heard praise and worship songs, and I fell completely in love with God. It was incredible. I can remember those songs as if I first heard them yesterday. After that, I visited another Christian church with a friend, and again I heard the Gospel and worship music. The song that caught my attention the most was about seeking first the Kingdom of God, and how then all things shall be added unto you. It was, in fact, that song that led me to the Lord. After the worship team sang it, and the pastor gave an altar call, I stood up with a face full of tears and walked down that aisle to receive Jesus into my heart. The song touched me and moved me. Singing it opened my eyes to see what I had been missing my whole life—Jesus. The song was taken straight from Matthew 6:33, and that has been my life verse ever since. Because of my conversion experience and the role worship played in it, I am a firm believer in worshiping God in spirit and in truth. I love connecting with God through song. Music often lifts us to a transcendent plane, and certainly one of worship's functions is to prepare us for heaven.

Worship is another secret sauce ingredient in parenting because it is foundational in building your children's lives for Jesus. Like prayer, worship in the lives of your children is essential because it reaches the *hearts* of your children for God. It is a two-way communication with God. In His Word, God speaks to us; in worship, we speak to God. Worship in song is powerful because it takes rhyme and rhythm and incorporates the truth of Scripture that we sing out to God. It reminds our souls of all that He has done. (Did you know that your soul, like a child, needs reminding? It absolutely does.)

Worship in parenting

The focus of worship for your children will be to get them to fall in love with Jesus as they look to the cross. When you saturate your home with worship, when you play it in the car or bring it up on TV and worship together as a family, something powerful happens in your children. It gets their eyes off of themselves and onto Jesus. It shows them how big God is, and how it's all about Him. When there are problems and hurdles in life, turn on the music and worship God with your kids. Show them that when you worship, walls come down, and the enemy flees.

As parents we get to take our children through life, and in times when we don't understand life, we get to say to them that one thing we do know is that God loves us, and He demonstrated His great love through the cross. When we see Jesus on the cross, we see His great love—His death for our sins and the amazing miracle of the resurrection. All of this was to give us life here on earth and eternal life—and that is when your children will fall in love with God the Father, God the Son, and God the Holy Spirit. That is when they will worship God in Spirit and in truth, when we will be one with God. They will experience the blessing of being in His presence, and that, my friend, is heaven here on earth!

Your whole life is worship!

Parents so often think that they're not doing a good job because they don't have time to spiritually lead their family every waking moment of the day. The truth is that if you love the Lord with all your heart, it will just come through in all that you do. When you're just going through your day, picking up your kids, taking time to listen to them, praying for them, dealing with people and situations in front of them in the Spirit and in love, not losing joy when something difficult happens—that's all worship! Your worship is your life, it is pointing them back to the heart of Jesus, and it is what is going to leave a lasting impact on your kids. When you have this mindset, you suddenly don't feel inadequate any longer. Your daily worship to God can be one long devotional to your kids. Don't ever forget that.

Insights from Sal

Throughout my childhood, my parents saturated my sister and me in worship songs. They even played them when we were in my mother's womb! No wonder we love worship music. Worship music brought me peace whenever I was feeling nervous. It took my eyes off the problems in life and lifted my eyes to the heavens. It taught me how to love the presence of God. It taught me to realize that when we worship, we disarm the enemy and make him flee. Growing up, I had the example of my parents going into a secret place, putting on worship music, and worshiping God with no one else to see. Just them and Him. There's nothing more beautiful and there's nothing more powerful than teaching your kids how to worship in the secret place. It will deepen their walk with the Lord so much. That's why my sister and I love to worship and why we became worship leaders. We love the presence of God so much that we want to lead others into His presence. Leading your kids to the cross and saturating them with worship will lead to an intimate relationship between them and Jesus. And that is the ultimate goal in parenting.

PUT IT INTO PRACTICE:
WORD, WORSHIP, PRAYER

- Be an example to your kids and be in the Word daily. Talk about it with your kids while you're eating your meals, driving in the car, shopping at the grocery store. Let it always be on your lips.

- Teach your kids how to read the Bible: conversationally, expectantly, obediently.

- Pray for your kids every single day and pray with them. Teach them how to pray (recite the actual words of the Lord's Prayer, *and* use it as a template). Show them how to search their hearts for idols and wrong heart attitudes. Teach them how to talk with the Lord as they would with a close friend, and give them the Word of God, which will help them fight off the enemy's attacks.

- Saturate your family's lives daily with worship. It will produce a natural love for worship so that they won't ever want to change the channel.

14

LEARN FROM OUR MISTAKES

The Way to Show GRACE to Your Kids

Aren't you beyond grateful for God's grace? Throughout my parenting journey, God has been showing me that in the same measure that I receive His unmerited, undeserved favor from Him, I must give it to my kids. Like all parents, I've made some mistakes in my parenting journey, but through it all, God showed me how grace can cover all of it. I want to share with you five practical, everyday ways to show grace to your kids, using the acronym GRACE.

G—Give your kids the capability to express their emotions.

How often do we, as parents, wake up on the wrong side of the bed feeling grumpy or moody or even hormonal? If we can have grace for ourselves when that happens, why shouldn't we have grace for our kids when they go through a bad day? Disclaimer: This isn't saying that you should let your kids disrespect you, but simply that there has to be an awareness and a tuning in to their emotions. They might be acting out because they had a hard day at school that they're not telling you about or because they're hungry or just plain tired. A lot of the time they aren't aware or can't communicate what's going on. So learn to be tuned in to them to figure it out. Ask the Holy Spirit to help you. Parents need to be intentional about creating a space where their children can open up about what's going on in their lives and how they're feeling. Little ones, especially around the toddler age, won't know how to express what they're feeling inside or struggling with. This is why parents need to create opportunities for conversations that will help them identify the needs of their children and equip them to face those needs. Let them express their emotions and learn how to respond, rather than react in anger or frustration. Lead by example in this area. Be open to your kids about how you feel. Say that you felt angry, sad, or fearful when you encountered such and such during your day. Your example will show them how to express their emotions. But the key is to not let yourself or them stay in those emotions. We shouldn't be stuck in our feelings (sorry, Drake) because our feelings come from our heart and our heart is deceitful and wicked above all else (see Jeremiah 17:9). Talk it through, make it clear to your kids that they should express their emotions but also that they should not be ruled or guided by them—it's their belief system that will dictate their emotions and thoughts. Make sure their beliefs are centered in the Word of God.

R—Raising your voice is not the way to communicate.

In my parenting journey, I found myself sometimes wanting to raise my voice in my home. Whenever I felt that urge come on, I would remind myself that you cannot be emotional and logical at the same time. I needed the Lord to help me transform my heart in this area. I had to learn to splash water on my face, or take a deep breath, or even go to another room and pray. Doing those things can make a world of difference. What really helped was the revelation that when I was responding impatiently, I was teaching my kids to do the same. I cannot overemphasize the importance of repenting to your kids. When your kids see you repenting about raising your voice, it will show them that raising their voice in anger or frustration is wrong and it's not something that is done in your house. Our kids learn the most when we repent to them. Show them that you were wrong and that God calls us to act in the Spirit and display patience and kindness and to be slow to speak. Also, if you want to be a healthy parent who raises healthy kids, you should regularly tell your kids that you want to grow in your parenting. Ask them what you and your spouse can improve on. It's a humbling question, and I have to warn you—you need to be willing to let your ego take a hit. But it is the most helpful question you could ask. As parents, we shouldn't be afraid to own our mistakes. We should be quick to apologize and quick to listen to feedback from our kids. This is how you and your whole family can grow.

A—Allow them to be creative.

One mistake that I made at the beginning of my parenting was allowing a little too much TV and technology for my kids. I didn't do this often, but it was more than I wanted to. I would put on a television show like *Barney* or *Sesame Street* or give them a Game Boy or video games to play. Now, that's not wrong for some of the time, but when it takes up all of their free time, it diminishes our children's ability to create. Television and iPad games do all of the creating for your kids, which is not engaging the part of the brain that lights up whenever creating happens. Instead, have your kids build a fort, or go out into the backyard and find certain types of birds and flowers and draw them. Once I started doing this more with my kids, I started to see them become more engaged and excited about life and less lazy and lethargic. Now my kids are some of the most creative people I have ever met—one is an inventor and engineer, and the other is the owner of a clothing company.

C—Converse positively about your kids.

Make sure the labels you put on your kids in passing conversations are not limiting, but empowering. Negative speaking can even be done unintentionally, like saying, "Sal is so shy" or "Sarah is such a picky eater." It might be said in passing, or without thought, but words are powerful, and your kids will take that to heart and let it become their identity. Speak life over them. Build them up. Tell them how intelligent they are and how kind they are. The enemy is an accuser who always tries to label us with the mistakes we've made so we'll take them on as our identity. If your kids make a mistake, be careful not to make it their identity by saying things like "You are selfish," "You're not smart," or "You're a liar." Rather, tell them they *acted* in those ways. Otherwise, when they blow it, they'll start to say to themselves, "I'm selfish," "I'm not smart," or "I'm a liar." That failure is not their identity. Remind them that they're not acting according to their identity—a child of God who walks in the fruit of the Spirit.

Speak faith over them. That's exactly what Ben Carson's mom did for him. Even when he was getting bad grades and not performing well in school, she still told him that he was too smart to be getting those grades and that he could do anything he set his mind to. Later on in his life, he became the world's most renowned neurosurgeon. (Mic drop.) Need I say more? Even the way we speak about them behind closed doors when they're not listening to us transforms *our* heart toward them. And what we say in front of them transforms their hearts. Praise your kids when they make the right decision to not give in to peer pressure, or when they change the channel if a bad commercial comes on. Give your children a steady diet of positive feedback and praise.

E—Encouraging, not fixing, is the most effective way.

As parents, sometimes we get into this mentality that we have to "fix" our kids rather than allow them to be who they are. This coincides with the chapter about not molding your kids but unfolding them. We shouldn't mold our kids into who we want them to be but let them become who God made them to be. We don't need to control every detail and aspect of their lives. They're going to get it figured out. God is not only our Shepherd but their Shepherd as well. Development and emotional maturity and independence are messy. Your children's growth is going to be messy and a massive roller coaster of ups and downs. Don't try to fix them, but rather encourage them and allow them to live as individuals. When we try to fix them, it will crush their spirit.

Looking back, I wish I'd had the mentality of a grandparent. How do I mean? We all know grandparents are much more relaxed than parents. They're way less uptight and have come to know the difference between what's precious and what's not. Instead of surviving their family, they're enjoying their family. This is the kind of perspective we need to have. We have to let go of control, let go of any ego attached to our parenting and simply let Jesus take the wheel (shout out to my girl Carrie Underwood).

Important reminder: Christ in you, the Hope of Glory. Here is the single redemptive reality that makes parenting possible: God in you! God knew that our calling would be so huge and our weakness so deep that the only thing that would help us was Himself. So, in an act of incredible grace, He has broken down our walls and come to live with us. Now think about this as a parent. This God who has the ability to do things that are beyond your ability to conceive, who has perfect wisdom and unlimited strength, right now lives inside of you. This means that God is with you in the morning when you dread getting out of bed and facing another hard parenting day. He is with you when you have to break up the squabbles each morning. He is with you when you fall into bed with a combination of exhaustion and regret. He is with you when you face illness, stress, fearful situations, joys, sadness—everything! He gifts you with His presence. He really does live inside you. You really aren't left to yourself. And He will be with you to the end of your parenting. What do you have as a Christian parent? You have God in every moment of every day. As parents we need to receive and believe this grace with all our hearts and give this grace to our children as well.

PUT IT INTO PRACTICE:
GRACE

- Write out your mistakes and make a mental note to be aware of these in your parenting. Be mindful of practicing GRACE:
  - Give your kids the capability to express their emotions.
  - Raising your voice is not the way.
  - Allow them to be creative.
  - Converse positively about your kids.
  - Encouraging, not fixing, is the most effective way.
- Something practical you can do to give your children the message of grace is to read the story of the prodigal son over and over to your children and say that this is what our heavenly Father does for us when we mess up, and that's what we do for you—give grace. Let them know that you're always going to be there with open arms. It will assure them that they can come to you about anything. Let your kids see how supported and loved they are, and no matter what decisions they've made, you will always guide them in the right direction. That support is so beautiful. Rather than trying to fix, you can pray and give grace.
- Set the tone for your home. Be a beacon of joy, light, peace, and calm for your family. Choose goodness

and excellence because you are an example to your family. Remember, parenthood is a marathon, not a sprint. You're never going to "arrive"—neither you nor them. The beauty of parenthood lies in the journey.

15

LEAVING A LEGACY OF FAITH

Raising Families the Kingdom Way

We started this journey of *Raising Families the Jesus Way* with my testimony on how Jesus saved my life (literally and spiritually). My life has been a journey of deep and radical faith, especially when it came to having my twin children, Sal and Sarah.

As mentioned previously, I was told I couldn't have kids. I had a medical diagnosis that meant it was almost impossible for me to get pregnant. My husband and I tried for years, but nothing ever happened. At that time, I was witnessing to my grandma, who was a professing Catholic. She was very devoted and went to mass every week, but still had some questions about a personal relationship with Jesus. I told my grandma, "Abuela, I'm going to prove to you that I have a personal relationship with Jesus, and as the Bible says, I can go directly to God and ask for a miracle to get pregnant." My grandma didn't think that would be a big enough miracle, so I went even more radical and told her I was going to pray for twins! She told me twins run in the family, so that wouldn't be that big of a miracle either. That was the last straw (my grandma was a tough cookie). I left it all on the table and told her our extended family had only ever had twins that were two girls or two boys, but I was going to pray a radical prayer for a boy and a girl! That finally got her attention, and she agreed with me that if that big miracle ever did happen, she would believe Jesus is the one and only Mediator to God.

That was when my faith started to kick into gear. I told the Lord, "Okay, God, I know You are a God of miracles, and I know You will come through." That was when the miracle happened: I got pregnant—with twins. But the story gets even better. Back in 1989, pagers were all the rage, Taylor Swift had just been born, and *Back to the Future Part II* had just come out. Also, hospital equipment was not as sophisticated as it is now, so when I went in to get my first sonogram, the doctor couldn't get a good read on the babies. They determined that one of them was a boy, but the other one, they had to measure the circumference of its head, and since the head was bigger than the other baby's head, they concluded that I was having two boys. I wouldn't believe it. I was so dead set that I was having a boy and a girl that I even started painting one half of our baby room blue and the other half pink. I bought all pink and blue clothes, and everyone I knew was telling me I was going to be very disappointed on delivery day. Nevertheless, I stood firm on my faith that I was going to have a boy and a girl, because that was what I was praying for in faith. I don't know where this crazy faith came from, but all the way to my delivery date I was filled with resolve and confidence that God was going to come through. And He did. I delivered baby number one . . . a boy, and then came baby number two . . . a girl! Everyone in the delivery room was shocked, including my husband, who actually fainted—twice! God came through, and my grandma ended up praying with us and asked the Holy Spirit to come fill her.

I tell this story because my children were born by a miracle that was rooted in faith. And throughout their upbringing, we taught them to live by faith and not by sight. Even when we were down to the last ten dollars in our bank account, in faith we gave our tithe to the Lord, telling our children that God would provide for us to buy groceries. God would always come through with random checks being left in our mailbox or groceries left on our doorstep. Not only have my husband and I lived by faith through radical miracles and tithing, but also by showcasing a profound and personal relationship with the Lord to our children. One of the nicest things anyone has ever said to me came from my daughter, Sarah, when she said, "Mom, I saw a quote on Instagram today and immediately thought of you." The quote, attributed to Charles Spurgeon, read: "A Bible that's falling apart usually belongs to someone who isn't." If anything, this is how we leave our children a legacy of faith. The heritage that I was leaving my children was seen, heard, and felt in the evidence of my profound and personal relationship with the Lord. My daughter knew my Bible was worn from use, evidence of a dependence on the Word of God. My children know my faith and my husband's faith is real because they've seen it lived out before their eyes. And that same faith has been instilled in them. Leaving a legacy of faith is just another way to sum up Deuteronomy 6:4–9, which says:

> Hear, O Israel: The LORD our God, the LORD is one. Love the LORD your God with all your heart and with all your soul and with all your strength. These commandments that I give you today are to be on your hearts. Impress them on your children. Talk about them when you sit at home and when you walk along the road, when you lie down and when you get up. Tie them as symbols on your hands and bind them on your foreheads. Write them on the doorframes of your houses and on your gates.

Living and leaving a legacy of faith instills a love for God beyond anything else, a desire for His Kingdom ways, and a laying up of treasures in heaven.

So, to all the parents and future parents reading this, what kind of legacy are you cultivating? I can say this with all certainty: You will never regret choosing to live for the Kingdom and building your life on faith. Don't waste your life and the lives of your children and grandkids by pursuing a legacy of vanity. God wants to bless our children, but we parents play an important role in this. Make sure you're planting yourself in the things of the Kingdom. We have the opportunity to prepare a place for them. Let's prepare them for the glorious Kingdom of God by seeking first His Kingdom: "But seek first the kingdom of God and His righteousness, and all these things shall be added to you" (Matthew 6:33 NKJV). Psalm 1 says that when you plant yourself in the Word and abide in Jesus, you will bear fruit and prosper, and more importantly, your children will prosper. This is how you leave a legacy of faith, how you raise families the Jesus way.

Insights from Sarah

One act of bold faith in your life can deliver to your future, and to your family's future, a legacy of faith that will be passed down to the next generation. If we leave nothing else behind, we must leave behind that legacy of faith. We have to leave behind a view that says we're not here to settle into what's comfortable or what's right in front of us. We're here to move on faith and believe that God's going to come through. Parents, it's great that you bless your kids and set them up financially. It's great if you're still married and if you're not passing down generational strongholds that they're going to have to fight through. That's all great. But the best thing that you can do is pass down a legacy of faith that says, "Mom and Dad did not play it safe with the Jesus that they came to know." In the Bible, we see that God chose Abraham to be the father of his people because He knew Abraham would teach his children His ways (see Genesis 18:19). God saw him as trustworthy. This directly shows that God is concerned about *legacy*.

My parents indeed passed down a legacy of faith to my brother and me. All throughout my life, they showed us what it was like to not play it safe, but instead to step out in bold faith. They tithed faithfully, even when they hardly had any money for the house payment. And the Lord came through for them every time. I saw them step out in faith by starting a church and building it from the ground up. I saw them start a business and go on missionary trips and pray over people to get healed. Their bold acts of faith not only inspired me to step out in faith in my own life, but showed me who Jesus really is. One does not simply step out in bold faith for a mediocre, religious God. My parents going head over heels into their faith showed me that Jesus is better than anything else this world can offer. Jesus is life, joy, peace, and freedom. That's someone I could go all in for.

Reflect the Heart of the Father

As we land the plane on this parenting journey, one very essential point we want to leave you with is this: *Reflect the heart of our heavenly Father toward your kids.* We know that God is love. Love not only provides for us but protects us, disciplines us, guides us, and frees us from bondage by refining and molding us.

The Bible says that God, our Father, is a perfect father, and when we have a relationship with Him, we get to experience His mercy, grace, and love. That is the way we're supposed to be with our children. He is the perfect father. If you didn't have a good father, you have your heavenly Father, who is the perfect example of what a father should be. Psalm 86:15 says, "But you, Lord, are a compassionate and gracious God, slow to anger, abounding in love and faithfulness." This is the heart that we need to reflect back to our kids. The Father's heart of love. This is how we can grow Kingdom families. Kingdom families are the only force that can swing back the pendulum of our culture toward what God intended it to be. God intends the family to be a blessing, a joy, a representation of the love relationship that He has with His children (you and me).

A Final Note of Encouragement

Godly parenting is about growing and raising the warriors of tomorrow. God has positioned your children strategically in this moment in history for a reason. Hidden inside of them, He has placed divine answers, solutions, and courage. Don't fear what could be in their future—just remind the enemy that he has to fear you. Keep going. And start *now* by leaving a legacy of faith for your children. Keep your faith rooted in this promise: He who began a good work in you (and in your children) will be faithful to complete it (see Philippians 1:6).

The Legacy Challenge

God has given us an "E-manual" to abide by in our parenting. In this manual (His Word), we find salvation, which changes the eternal destiny of our kids. We also find how to have the indwelling of the Holy Spirit, which brings transformation to our kids. Our part is to lead our children to the Lord, guide them by the Word of God, and use resources to water and nurture them into what God has called them to be. Let's take His Word and the Holy Spirit's guidance to heart and leave a lasting legacy for our children and for generations to come.

Let this eulogy be the legacy we leave our children.

God's Word was their E-manual.

They lived and moved and breathed God's Word and built a strong foundation for their family, centered on the Word of God.

They shared the Gospel with their children and led them to the Lord.

They modeled Christ for their children, lived out the Bible's instructions, and mirrored godly character to them.

They forgave others and exemplified a godly image to their children.

They blessed them and led their family to the cross.

They cared enough to address sin in their children's lives and disciplined them according to the Word because they loved them.

They got rid of generational patterns and let the Holy Spirit heal their hearts and minds so that they could focus on parenting the hearts of their children.

They led their homes in spiritual leadership and discipleship.

They unfolded their children's God-given gifts and used practical strategies to raise their kids with godly character.

They partnered with the Holy Spirit to parent by the Spirit of God.

And ultimately, they covered their children in prayer, worship, and the Word until their dying breath.

This is how we can go back to the future and change the world for generations to come. Through a legacy of faith.

I have no greater joy than to hear that my children are walking in the truth.

3 John 1:4

NOTES

Chapter 1 Back to the Bible

1. Kturton, "How does a seed know what to grow into?," Simple Scimum, September 3, 2016, https://simplescimum.wordpress.com/2016/09/03/how -does-a-seed-know-what-to-grow-into/.

Chapter 2 Essentials for Parenting the Jesus Way

1. Lusko, Levi Lusko, "Preparing Your Children to Spread Their Wings | Pastor Levi Lusko | La Familia Part 3/3," YouTube, 25 July 2022, https:// www.youtube.com/watch?v=Ot6MwsA2X7Q.

2. Tony Evans, *One Family Under God: Preserving the Home as God Intended* (Chicago: Moody Publishers, 2013), 7–9.

3. Nate Johnson, "The days of building empires is over," Facebook, March 16, 2022, https://www.facebook.com/natejamesjohnston/posts/pfbid0H3ePzn7ytyv WCSQbbuGsPBHJPydv7CDu2vs6fQSVgUxg9HaXZEon16iYPasa7dtKl.

4. "Would You Like to Know God Personally?" Cru, https://www.cru .org/us/en/how-to-know-god/would-you-like-to-know-god-personally.html.

Chapter 4 Too Blessed to Be Stressed

1. Children's Bureau, "A Father's Impact on Child Development," citing *Psychology Today*, allforkids.org, June 7, 2018, https://www.all4kids.org /news/blog/a-fathers-impact-on-child-development/.

2. Mark Twain, 1906 letter to Gertrude Natkin, quoted on TwainQuotes .com, "Compliment," http://www.twainquotes.com/Compliment.html.

Chapter 5 I'm Going to Tell My Kids . . .

1. Caroline Leaf, *Switch on Your Brain* (Grand Rapids, MI: Baker House, 2015), 59.

2. Daniel Amen, "The Most Important Lesson from 83,000 Brain Scans," TED Summaries, April 15, 2014, https://tedsummaries.com/2014/04/17/the -most-important-lesson-from-83000-brain-scans-daniel-amen.

Chapter 6 The Heart of the Problem

1. Tedd Tripp, *Shepherding a Child's Heart, Revised and Updated* (Wap-wallopen, PA: Shepherd Press, 1995), 6.

Chapter 8 As for Me and My House

1. "Give Me Liberty Or Give Me Death!" Colonial Williamsburg, https://www.colonialwilliamsburg.org/learn/deep-dives/give-me-liberty-or-give-me -death.

2. "Franklin D. Roosevelt, Inaugural Address Online," published by Gerhard Peters and John T. Woolley, The American Presidency Project, https://www.presidency.ucsb.edu/documents/inaugural-address-8.

3. "John F. Kennedy Inaugural Address Online," published by Gerhard Peters and John T. Woolley, The American Presidency Project, https://www .presidency.ucsb.edu/documents/inaugural-address-2.

4. "Never Give In, Never, Never, Never, 1941," America's National Churchill Museum, https://www.nationalchurchillmuseum.org/never-give-in-never-never -never.html.

5. Quote in Olivia B. Waxman, "Lots of People Have Theories About Neil Armstrong's 'One Small Step for Man' Quote. Here's What We Really Know," *Time*, July 15, 2019, https://time.com/5621999/neil-armstrong-quote.

6. Sandra Stanley, "An Intentional Parenting Strategy for Andy and Sandra Stanley," Focus on the Family, 2017, https://www.focusonthefamily.com /parenting/an-intentional-parenting-strategy-for-andy-and-sandra-stanley.

7. Richard Dugdale, *The Jukes: A Study of Crime, Pauperism, Disease and Heredity*, 5th ed. (New York: Putnam and Sons, 1891), http://readingroom .law.gsu.edu/cgi/viewcontent.cgi?article=1000&context=buckvbell.

8. Albert E. Winship, *Jukes-Edwards: A Study in Education and Heredity* (Harrisburg, PA: R. L. Myers, 1900), https://www.biodiversitylibrary.org /bibliography/25046.

9. Stan and Brenna Jones, *The Story of Me* (Colorado Springs: Navpress, 2007).

10. This quote is often attributed to Mother Teresa.

Chapter 9 Don't Mold, Unfold

1. Quoted in Pat Williams, *Coach Wooden: The 7 Principles That Shaped His Life and Will Change Yours* (Grand Rapids, MI: Revell 2011), 178.

2. Attributed to John Wooden. Original source material unknown.

3. Kristi Noem, in 2019 South Dakota Inaugural: The inauguration of Governor Kristi Noem, 33rd Governor State of South Dakota, West Palm Beach Convention, January 5, 2019, Pierre, SD, Pierre Area Chamber of Commerce.

4. Haley Sweetland Edwards, "Boundless Mind Wants to Fix America's Smartphone Addiction," *Time*, April 29, 2021, https://time.com/5237434 /youre-addicted-to-your-smartphone-this-company-thinks-it-can-change -that.

Chapter 10 Legos and Kitchens

1. Lisa Bevere, "Mothers Day with Special Guest Lisa Bevere," Sandals Church, May 8, 2020, Riverside, CA, https://sandalschurch.com/watch/mothers -day-with-special-guest-lisa-bevere.

2. "About Teen Pregnancy," Centers for Disease Control and Prevention, November 15, 2021, https://www.cdc.gov/teenpregnancy/about/index.htm.

3. Suzanne Wymelenberg, "The Dilemma of Teenage Parenthood," *Science and Babies: Private Decisions, Public Dilemmas* (Washington, D.C.: National Academies Press, 1990), chap. 4, https://www.ncbi.nlm.nih.gov /books/n/nap1453/ddd00061.

Chapter 11 The Chastened Child

1. Jon Courson, "The Chastened Child-Part 1 Hebrews 12:5-11 - Jon Courson," YouTube, November 3, 2017, https://www.youtube.com/watch? v=AIIrPnau8go.

2. "Dr. Benjamin Spock's Influence and Controversy," Study.com, September 15, 2021, https://study.com/academy/lesson/dr-benjamin-spock-bio graphy-theories.html.

Chapter 12 Holy Spirit–Led Parenting

1. Chip Judd, *Boundaries: A Key To Healthy Relationships*, audio cassette, www.amazon.com/Boundaries-Healthy-Relationships-Chip-Judd/dp /B002QUTZJ4.

2. Judd, *Boundaries*, www.amazon.com/Boundaries-Healthy-Relation ships-Chip-Judd/dp/B002QUTZJ4.

Chapter 13 The Secret Sauce

1. Chuck Missler, "The Gospel in Genesis: A Hidden Message," Koinonia House, February 1, 1996, https://www.khouse.org/articles/1996/44.

Mary Garcia has a master's degree in marriage and family counseling, has been a certified biblical and family counselor for thirty years, and is a family pastor. Her passion is to share deep and rich wisdom from her life experiences and biblical insights on how to raise godly children. She is a pastor's wife and has led and spoken at many women's events throughout the years. She has also been a professor at a Bible college, where she taught marriage and family courses. Mary loves to impart wisdom and truth from her life experiences to the younger generation.

Sarah Garcia has a master's degree in counseling ministry and is a certified youth and family counselor. She has a passion for counseling and discipling junior high and high school girls. She also counsels her generation as well as sharing with the older generation on how to restore broken relationships in their families. She owns a successful faith-based clothing business called Glorify Apparel, which has an international reach. Sarah is a natural-born writer and has impacted many people through her blogs, social media posts, and church curriculum.

Sal Garcia has a double master's degree in computer and electrical engineering, is an inventor with several patents, works for various major consumer electronics companies as a senior engineer, and has fifteen years of experience discipling young men. Sal is a teacher at heart and loves to take complicated topics and make them easy to understand. His wisdom and insight in this book will bring so much guidance and foreknowledge to young parents.

Frank Garcia has been married to Mary for 36 years. He has been involved in ministry for over forty years, pastoring churches and counseling couples and families. He has developed and teaches materials that encourage families to parent with the heart in mind. He has also taught men's ministry seminars that help fathers be leaders in their homes. Frank's passion is to shepherd the flock and raise up godly families in today's world.